HUMAN ECOLOGY

A
Physician's Advice
for
Human Life

Robert L. Jackson, M.D.

Professor Emeritus
Department of Child Health
University of Missouri
Columbia, Missouri

Professor of Pediatrics
University of Kansas
Kansas City, Kansas

ST. BEDE'S PUBLICATIONS
Petersham, Massachusetts

St. Bede's Publications
P.O. Box 545, North Main Street
Petersham, MA 01366-0545

97   96   95   94   93   92   91   90   5   4   3   2   1

Nihil Obstat:
   Most Reverend Charles H. Helmsing
   Censor Deputatus Librorum
   August 22, 1989

Imprimatur:
   Most Reverend John J. Sullivan
   Bishop of Kansas City-St. Joseph
   August 22, 1989

The *Nihil Obstat* and *Imprimatur* are official declarations that a book
or pamphlet is free of doctrinal and moral error. No implication is
contained therein that those granting the *Nihil Obstat* and *Imprimatur*
agree with the content, opinions or statements expressed.

LIBRARY OF CONGRESS CATALOGING-IN-PUBLICATION DATA

Jackson, Robert L., 1909-
    Human ecology : a physician's advice for human life / Robert L.
Jackson
          p.   cm.
    Includes bibliographical references.
    ISBN 0-932506-75-5
    1. Family--Health and hygiene. 2. Natural family planning.
3. Breast feeding. 4. Christian life--1960-   I. Title.
    [DNLM: 1. Breast Feeding. 2. Catholicism. 3. Family Planning.
4. Religion and Medicine.   HQ 766.3 J13h]
RA418.5.F3J33   1990
241'.63--dc20
DNLM/DLC for Library of Congress   90-8926
                                                          CIP

Dedication

To Mary, woman of faith and perseverance, and all women who imitate her. Mary, the daughter of the Father, the spouse of the Holy Spirit and the mother of Jesus, our Redeemer.

To Sarah Elizabeth Soisson, my spouse for over fifty years and the mother of our six daughters and son. Her commitment and daily life as wife and mother have taught me and our children faith, hope and love.

To Ann, Mary Jo, Sally, Kathy, Margy, Martha, Bobby and their spouses, who in Christian marriages as co-creators, have given us six granddaughters and twelve grandsons.

CHAPTERS

Foreword

At the University of Iowa, Dr. Robert Jackson developed the Iowa Growth Charts, which became national and international standards for evaluating the growth and maturation of infants and children. Since all infants included in the study were "well-born" and favored by their environment, these standards came to be regarded as the optimal norms for pediatric practice.

In 1934, Dr. Jackson began his postgraduate studies in Pediatrics at the University of Iowa Nutrition Center, under the direction of Drs. P. C. Jeans and G. Stearns. Jeans and Stearns developed the first infant and child metabolic research unit, which was a precursor to the clinical research centers which now exist in many research institutions in our country. Research done at the Iowa Pediatric Nutrition Center contributed to improved methods for modifying and preparing cow's milk formulas as well as to determining the kinds and amounts of vitamins and minerals needed for supplementation. Observations from this and other research centers gradually extended our knowledge of the nutritional requirements of infants and children for optimal growth and development. As an expert in infant and child nutrition, Dr. Jeans served for many years both on the Council on Foods and Nutrition of the American Medical Association and on the Food and Nutrition Board of the National Research Council. After his retirement, the author succeeded him in these appointments.

In the study at the Iowa Pediatric Nutrition Center, many of the infants were either breast-fed with bottle supplements or bottle-fed. Consequently, in 1964 at the University of Missouri, Columbia, the growth of groups of "well-born" infants who were fed only human milk was compared to the growth of infants who were fed modified and supplemented cow's milk formulas. The growth curves for body length throughout the first six months of all infants in the study were found to be almost identical to the Iowa norms. One subgroup of breast-fed infants received *no* supplemental vitamins or additional foods. The pattern of growth in body length for both sexes in this subgroup also was remarkably similar to the Iowa norms, with only a slightly less rapid weight gain (especially in the boys) during the later months. This slightly less rapid weight gain may well be more "normal" or physiological.

These studies stimulated Dr. Jackson to define what constitutes a well-born or well endowed child and how best to assist nature to attain and maintain optimal health and well-being of mothers and their children.

Environmentalists and ecologists are becoming more aware that actions affecting one aspect of nature frequently have effects far more widespread than had previously been suspected. Ecology is the branch of biology dealing with living organisms, their habits and mutual relationship to their environment. The recent interest in ecology has centered primarily upon the effects that man's actions have on the subhuman world of air, water, plants and animals. Too little attention has been directed to human ecology.

For example, the major factor which led to shortened child-spacing was the gradual displacement of breast-feeding by bottle feeding. Artificial (bottle) feeding resulted in early postpartum ovulation and to abnormally shortened child-spacing of about one year, and consequently to overwhelming physical, emotional and economic stress on families. These family stresses induced couples in Western societies to seek means for controlling the frequency of conceptions. The general unreliability of and the self-discipline required by the so-called "calendar rhythm method," and the easy availability and convenience of unnatural methods which were advised by professionals, readily persuaded most couples to use artificial methods of conception regulation. A natural technique of regulating births relies on nature in order to take advantage of the fact that women have only a very limited time of fertility within the menstrual cycle. In contrast, the unnatural methods provide a technique for distorting the sexual act or study nature in order to determine how to cause a distruption of human reproductive biology, usually in the female, so that the normal act of intercourse will no longer cause conception, or if conception does occur, the pregnancy will be aborted.

Human attitudes are changing, and an increasing number of concerned young people are seeking a more natural and less artificial way of life. Many artificial practices insidiously adopted in recent decades are being reappraised, such as those associated with childbirths. Few people realize that the large-scale change from natural childbirth and natural (breast) feeding to unnatural methods of childbirth and infant feeding took place only within the present century. Unnatural methods of childbirth are those which constitute an unwarranted medical or surgical intervention in an uncomplicated delivery.

In the present century, advances in scientific knowledge have occurred at a rate faster than our ability to appraise and apply them to the welfare of man. Children deserve to be "well-born" and "well-raised". We can foresee ways to ultimately approximate this goal. To be well-born, an infant needs a healthy mother for its nine months of intrauterine life. To be well-raised, the child needs an enduring family. However, to achieve these goals, we must not only apply new knowledge more effectively, we must also address the underlying problems of social and economic instability. Moreover, we need to revise and extend maternal and child health programs so as to obtain and maintain higher degrees of health. In other words, we need to focus much greater attention on preventive maternal, paternal and child care.

In the early 1900s, maternal and child health educational programs began to evolve in the U.S.A. After the first World War, the American Red Cross began to offer instructions to mothers for improving their health during pregnancy and providing better care for their infants after birth. In the 1920s and 1930s, many other governmental and private agencies began developing maternal and child health educational and clinic services. Mothers were urged to seek prenatal care to prevent complications during pregnancy and to make it possible for doctors to detect early symptoms and signs of impending problems. Increased knowledge, especially in nutrition, bacteriology and pharmacology made it possible to prevent, as well as to treat, infectious diseases which in the past killed so many infants and children. Before this time it was not uncommon for families to lose about as many children as they were able to raise to adult life.

Pediatrics evolved rapidly as a medical specialty during this period, and many infant care centers became available to monitor the growth and development of infants and preschool children and to detect earlier signs of illness. Pediatrics led the way by giving ever-increasing attention to preventive medical care in order to raise the level of health of our most valuable resource—our children. In these pages, Dr. Jackson has distilled more than fifty years of experience as a pediatrician. The information presented here is grounded in current scientific research; at the same time it offers an integrated vision for the care of humans from conception to young adulthood. In the fullest sense, it is about human ecology.

Preface

In this book, the author, a distinguished physician, offers a blueprint for the reconstruction of our society by proposing a way of life that will bring true meaning, fulfillment and maturity to its members. It is a proposal which takes into account the ethical dimension of life; the maturing of adults; the mental and emotional welfare of children; and the populating of the West with the children and adults which it needs to survive. His first regard is for the family, the basic unit of society. He brings to his proposal current research findings little known by those who will profit most from them: adults and families, doctors and health-care workers, private, corporate, and government planners. These findings are distilled through the experience of fifty years of a distinguished medical career, as well as fifty years of marriage, during which time he and his wife raised seven children who are now married and have numerous children.

As Pope Paul VI foresaw in his 1968 encyclical *Humanae Vitae*, contraception has inevitably led to the problems we face today: promiscuity, abortion, euthanasia, the degradation of women, the spread of venereal diseases and to what the Pope did not foresee explicitly, the deadly AIDS epidemic. Human dignity has been assaulted and the worth of human lives has been ignored as a result of detaching human sexuality from its naturally determined role of procreation, which deepens the union of spouses who together value human life.

Our society seems to have given up on self-control and self-discipline in important areas. Self-control is admittedly difficult for adolescents, especially if they lack proper training in a loving family and live in a culture which does not esteem these values. Today many social forces, including television, the media, and the adult world, tend to undermine self-discipline. Many of the programs of sex education to which our children are subjected introduce them to and encourage promiscuity ("sexual activity"), instead of educating them in responsibility. By providing children with condoms and birth control pills instead of teaching abstinence and self-control, our society is exposing its adolescents to the fatal plague of AIDS.

To modify this situation, Dr. Jackson proposes a natural way of life. He encourages the education of children in a manner that promotes this way of life, including training in self-discipline in preparation for marriage. He advises natural fertility testing of the newly married, natural childbirth, breast-feeding for at least one year, and natural family planning.The results, experience has shown, are the increasing maturity of adults, the greater stability of marriage with increased communication and cooperation between partners, better health and human development of infants and children, and more self-giving families. In this direction lies a renewed society.

Underlying the movement of which Dr. Robert Jackson is such a significant part is the philosophy of Dr. Herbert Ratner, former Health Commissioner of Oak Park, Illinois and Professor at Loyola Medical College, and present Visiting Professor of New York Medical College and editor of the journal Child and Family. Dr. Ratner sees the replacement of natural effective ways of living by destructive artificial ways as a failure to respect God, our Father and Creator, who has established in nature a pattern which we can choose to reject only at great cost. For, as he often says in his talks on different continents, "Whereas God always forgives, and man sometimes forgives, nature never forgives."

To live a truly natural life requires grace. Divine help is needed to do so. This help is forthcoming to those who ask for it, and who are willing to pursue a life pleasing to God. Such a spiritual life strengthens one's determination to respect God the Creator and Father and the order He has established. It increases the psychological resources of the person and leads to meaning and fulfillment in life, despite its inevitable difficulties and sorrows. Such a life increases mental health and helps to prevent or ameliorate mental and emotional illness, the depressions, anxieties, phobias and impulse disorders so common today.

Dr. Jackson looks forward to a peaceful and just society into which today's adults can introduce the properly conceived and developed children upon whom our future depends.

Fr. Raphael Simon, O.C.S.O., M.D.
St. Joseph's Abbey
Spencer, Mass 01562

Editor's Note: Fr. Simon has developed the themes mentioned above in: **Hammer and Fire. Way to Contemplative Happiness, Fruitful Apostolate and Mental Health**, *available from St. Bede's Publications.*

Acknowledgments

I would like to thank many people—more than can be named in this space—who directly and indirectly have contributed to the making of this book, including the artist Edna Hibel, who painted the Holy Family for the frontispiece. I especially want to thank the following contributors and reviewers of the manuscript: Herbert Ratner, M.D., of Oak Park, Illinois, Visiting Professor of Community and Preventive Medicine, New York Medical College, New York, and renowned editor of the periodical *Child and Family*. For over thirty years under Ratner's editorship, *Child and Family* has espoused the advantages of a natural way of life. Thank you, Herb, for your friendship, your wisdom and for your willingness to write the epilogue of this book. I would also like to thank Hanna Klaus, M.D., Clinical Professor of Obstetrics and Gynecology of George Washington University and Director of the Natural Family Planning Center, Washington, D.C.; Thomas Hilgers, M.D., Clinical Professor of Obstetrics and Gynceology, Creighton University, Omaha, Nebraska and Director of the Pope Paul VI Institute for the Study of Human Reproduction; John Billings, M.D. and Lyn Billings, M.D. of Melbourne Australia, authors of the Ovulation Method of Natural Family Planning; Peter Howie, M.D. and associates of Dundee, Scotland, for granting permission to reprint the illustrations used in Chapter 5; John and Sheila Kippley of Cincinnati, Ohio, founders of the "Couple to Couple League" and authors of the excellent teaching manual, *The Art of Natural Family Planning,* which includes and stresses the importance of ecological breast-feeding; Father Raphael Simon, M.D., of Saint Joseph's Abbey, Spencer, Massachusetts for his encouragement and for writing the preface of this book; Father Richard

Huneger of Portland, Oregon, Archdiocesan Director of Pastoral Services, and Father Philip Kraus, S.J., of Irvington, New Jersey, National Director of Diocesan Development Program for Natural Family Planning, for their critical reviews and contributions to the text; Mother Mary Clare and Sister Mary Joseph of St. Bede's Publications for their helpful suggestions and for publishing the manuscript. The author also wishes to thank Mary Shivanandan, of Bethesda, Maryland, Director of K.M. Associates and a recognized author in the field of human sexuality, for her assistance in the final shaping and editing of this manuscript.

In acknowledging the help of all of these friends and supporters, I must also mention my family and professional associates who for many years, have been supportive and tolerant of an "alleged" author in their midst. One day one of my young adult grandsons picked up a copy of the manuscript. After reading for a few minutes, he said, "You know, grandpa, this is really interesting and no doubt true, but do you think that the young people of today will accept your old fashioned ideas and advice?" I replied that truth does not change nor is it found by taking public opinion polls. To a great extent, truth is recognized by trial and error and ultimately comes to be known as wisdom. I also told him that as a pediatrician I had learned early in my clinical practice that what most parents and grandparents in every generation will do for their children is beyond human understanding, and consequently I had great confidence and hope for the long term future of families.

Introduction

It is a great honor to be given the opportunity to write the introduction to this book. The author, Robert L. Jackson, M.D., is eminently qualified to write this book and to provide the insights it contains. He has experienced most of life's dimensions in a loving and caring fashion, including its medical and physiological aspects as they relate to the ecology of the human person and to the family. He has been concerned with these aspects in research, medical practice, and teaching.

As a founding member of the Pediatric Endocrine Society and for many years a council member of the American Diabetes Association, Dr. Jackson was awarded the Banting Medal in 1969, the highest honor of the ADA. In 1974 the Association also gave him their first special award for his "untiring services on behalf of diabetic youth." Dr. Jackson is an expert in the use of hormones for children with endocrine disorders, as well as in the areas of natural living treated in this book.

We are experiencing great social difficulty as we enter the 1990s. Much of that difficulty has come about as the result of our ignoring human ecology, by ignoring those principles which keep in proper balance the orderly development of the human family and the resulting human person.

Dr. Jackson outlines an approach which is medically and physiologically sound, yet is barely understood by many of our medical colleagues. Medical education in the Western world, with its major emphasis on technology, virtually overlooks the innate sacred value and dignity of the human person.

Many of the medical and physiological insights contained in this book have been gleaned from the long tradition of philosophical and theological discourse which has taken place under the guidance of the Catholic Church. Unfortunately, for whatever reasons, those philosophical and theological perspectives and insights have been bypassed by the medical profession at large, with a resultant loss to the welfare of human society.

I hope that people read this book with the perspective of a *new framework* within which we, in the medical field, can view the human person. This book is not anti-technological. Technology is not all bad! But technology in the absence of a basic respect for the value and dignity of the human person can be destructive. This book places the emphasis where it belongs: on the value and dignity of the human person.

We live in a society where divorce is on the increase exponentially; contraception and abortion are so common that they have numbed our nation's conscience; paradoxically, there has been an increase in out-of-wedlock pregnancies, in the exploitation of both men and women through graphic pornography, in physical and sexual child abuse, in drug abuse, in teen-age suicide, in homosexuality, in artificial reproduction through artificial insemination by husband and by donor and in *in vitro* fertilization, and in other dehumanizing forms of reproductive technology. We exist in an age where family violence is epidemic and truly out of control.

Through the concepts of human ecology elaborated in this most significant book, Dr. Jackson lays out a blueprint for "resetting" the human family and alleviating many of these problems.

This book touches upon human sexual ecology in many different ways, ways, indeed, for which I am personally grateful. It is intrinsically important for us both as men and women to be able to properly balance our human sexuality. An ecologically sensitive human sexual equilibrium is only possible in the context of natural conception regulation, usually referred to as natural family planning. The provision of such services requires a person-oriented concern for the human family and a willingness to reach out in a way that makes a difference.

I hope that this book will make a difference. I truly hope that physicians, especially obstetricians-gynecologists, family practitioners, and pediatricians, will take seriously the mounting data on family violence that is clearly outlined in Chapter 10, and realize the role that they as physicians play in contributing to this violence and the role which they can play in its solution.

I share Dr. Jackson's concern about the "moral vacuum" which "is enveloping our civilization." But I also share Dr. Jackson's belief that there are movements today for a "return to values and practices that have held families together and contributed to a more stable society; that is, a sense of personal responsibility and dignity, including chastity before and fidelity after marriage." And that "a return to natural family planning in all of its aspects offers the best hope of overcoming the sense of foreboding for the future."

Please pick up this book and read it! Read it with a sense of openness and a sense of refreshment. Read it with a sense of peace, and understand that the author, in his generosity and kindness (and with intellectual and academic excellence) is asking you to look at the human family once again as a unit best nurtured and developed in the context of love, respect, dignity, and balance.

Thomas W. Hilgers, M.D., FACOG, CNFPE
Senior Medical Consultant,
Obstetrics, Gynecology and Reproductive Medicine Director,
Pope Paul VI Institute For the Study of Human Reproduction

Chapter 1

Natural Childbirth

Parents have gradually been led to believe that doctors deliver babies rather than that mothers give birth. It is sad that so many American parents so fear labor and birth that they choose a surgical removal of their child. Despite the efforts of some doctors and nurses to advocate natural births, many mothers continue to come to labor poorly informed. They are separated from their families or close friends and deprived of the support of those who, if trained, could help them the most.

A combination of factors contributes to many parents being told that the mother should have a caesarean for the safety of the baby. The increased use of mechanical rather than clinical monitoring tends to invite intervention. When the physician considers progress too slow, something is given or done to hurry the process; if labor seems too rapid, something is given or done to retard the progress. These practices foster an attitude that regards mothers as being unable to give birth without intervention.

In Western societies, home deliveries prevailed before the 1930s. The husband and grandmother were usually present to reassure the mother, to assist the midwife, and to notify the family doctor in time to attend, if need be, the birth of the baby. However, in the second quarter of this century, doctors began urging mothers to have sterile hospital deliveries. This made it possible for doctors and nursing staff to supervise a greater number of women more closely, and to have access to whatever equipment might be needed to manage mothers with complications. Consequently, methods and procedures of childbirth changed rapidly, and soon most mothers with or without impending problems were hospitalized. Labor and delivery procedures were defined and supervised by specialists in the obstetrical section of the hospital.

most mothers with or without impending problems were hospitalized. Labor and delivery procedures were defined and supervised by specialists in the obstetrical section of the hospital.

The rapid change from home births to hospital deliveries had many advantages for women needing special attention, but it also had disadvantages for healthy women not needing intervention. Perinatal and infant death rates rapidly decreased with improved medical care. Although hospitalization and advances in technology tended to dehumanize the birth event and to complicate modes of living, these changes also prevented the greater tragedies of maternal and infant deaths which were commonplace a century ago. We need to realize that for about every hundred babies born at the turn of the century, one mother died.

The responsibility for natural birth was gladly given up by most nineteenth century women, who understandably wanted to be relieved of pain during labor and delivery. "Twilight sleep" was introduced in the early part of this century. This morphine-scopolamine combination allowed mothers to undergo labor in a dreamy, narcotized condition, but the trance-like state made it more difficult for the mother to deliver her baby unaided, with the result that more and more healthy women required or were given various forms of obstetrical assistance.

As improved anesthetic agents became available centuries, birth gradually became a medical event requiring various forms of intervention. More recently, with the availability of sophisticated monitoring methods, birth is no longer merely a medical event: it is now also a surgical event. Every doctor wants pregnant women under his or her supervision to have a perfect baby. This goal, coupled with the current teaching in most medical schools of indications for caesarean operations (a teaching which is reinforced during most internships and residencies), accounts for the alarmingly high number of caesarean births. Parents expect a "perfect baby" and thus are unprepared to accept the inevitability of occasional morbidity and mortality accompanying the birth event. As a result, many obstetricians increasingly proceed to surgical intervention to lessen the likelihood of litigation. The astronomically rising cost of malpractice insurance in the United States is causing increasing numbers of some well-trained and experienced obstetricians to reject deliveries of "high-risk" mothers—the very mothers who need their help the most. On the positive side, the high insurance rates are also triggering the withdrawal from obstetric practice of many doctors less competent to manage high-risk mothers.

Women eagerly accepted what many considered "liberation from biological oppression," but over a period of thirty to forty years, obstetricians and pediatricians have begun to realize that for a normal birth, the danger of methods used to relieve pain have often far outweighed the benefits both for the mother and her baby.

The first major attempt to cope with labor pains by other than chemical means was made in Russia in the early 1900s. The conditioned character of pain was first demonstrated in 1912; as a result, the inevitability of intolerable pain in childbirth began to be questioned. The new method of "pain management" was called psychopropylaxis, indicating the prevention of pain by psychological means.[1] In 1951, the French obstetrician Dr. F. Lamaze visited Russia and subsequently introduced the method into Europe.[2] This method was popularized in the United States in 1959 when Marjorie Karmel published a book entitled *Thank you, Dr. Lamaze*.[3]

In the 1920s, Dr. Dick-Read, a medical practitioner in Birmingham, England, independently observed that women who expected little pain gave birth with relative ease. In 1933, he published his book, *Natural Childbirth*, which indicated how fear interfered with the natural contractions of the uterus during labor.[4] In the 1950s, Drs. Thoms and Karlowski also published studies done at Yale University on natural childbirth,[5] and in 1969 Dr. Bonica published a detailed discussion of the various strategies used for controlling pain in his textbook *Principles and Practice of Obstetric Analgesia and Anesthesia*.[6]

Dr. Mayer Eisenstein recently published a book entitled *The Home Court Advantage*, reviewing in considerable detail the advantages of natural childbirth for healthy mothers.[7] Among his list of inspirational birthing teachers, he states "I must mention the guru of all home birth gurus, Dr. Herbert Ratner. Dr. Ratner was a general practitioner for years, a professor of philosophy at Loyola University and the teacher of my mentor, Dr. Gregory White. Dr. White taught me the art and science of home deliveries. Dr. Ratner arranged to have his son-in-law, Dr. George Dietz, spend time teaching me obstetrics on his day off when I was a resident."

All natural methods of childbirth that evolved were based upon education and psychological support for the mother during labor and delivery. Natural childbirth is a highly structured method based upon the mother's conditioning and concentration, and thus it requires self-discipline. The mother must assume an active role in the learning process, as well as the responsibility for preserving and maintaining active participation throughout labor and delivery. The mothers who have been most successful are those who have had the support of a coach, not only during the training period, but also continuously during labor and delivery. A mature, trained husband has been found to be very effective, but because of the need for dependability and experience, more often another caring, trained and experienced person is preferable, especially for the birth of a first child.

It is well documented that when a concerned person supports the mother during labor, through breathing techniques, relaxation, and other amenities, she is then usually able to accept and maintain control of the normal process; but when that support is disrupted or absent, the contractions are more likely to be perceived as painful, and invariably she begins to request help to suppress the pains.[8]

Cultural and familial support has gradually become less available in Western society. For one thing, many couples live far away from their families, most of their mothers had non-natural hospital obstetrical deliveries, and most never successfully breast-fed their infants.

The concept of "family-centered maternity care" has been present for more than a quarter of a century, but until recently it has been ineffectively implemented. However, because of consumer demands, many hospitals in the 1980s are currently re-evaluating their policies in this regard. One of the positive aspects of the women's movement has been to accelerate these changes and to alter women's concept of themselves during childbirth. Clinical evidence has been accumulating to demonstrate that many childbirth practices actually interfere with the welfare of both the mother and her baby. Concomitantly, there has been a growing awareness of both the emotional aspects of childbirth and of the critical time, soon after birth, when a natural "bonding" takes place between the mother and her newborn infant.[9]

Family-centered maternity care that includes "rooming-in" now enables many mothers and fathers to become acquainted with their child immediately after birth. More and more informed young couples are questioning the need for the escalating costs of hospital deliveries of healthy mothers by medical specialists. The rise in consumerism has encouraged people to demand a more active role in all the important events of their lives including the child-bearing experience. Until recently, most doctors and hospitals were not responsive to change. The almost universal use of drugs and anesthetics during labor and delivery made it necessary for the mother to have custodial care. Hospital admission procedures usually required removal of clothing and personal belongings, and often entailed separation from family members. The demoralizing effect of these procedures has led to the demand for a return to a more natural and humanized birth experience,[10] including supervised home deliveries or childbirth centers located in or near a hospital (in case of unexpected complications) and home-like hospital birthing rooms.[11]

Birth is a very significant experience for all concerned. Obstetricians and pediatricians have extended and provided scientific knowledge, and greatly improved medical care for mothers with complications and for infants with problems.

Obstetricians firmly believe in the appropriateness and necessity of what they do, and through their efforts during this century, we have almost eliminated maternal deaths. Likewise, pediatricians have helped improve the life expectancy of newborn infants, especially those born prematurely.

However, many problems arise when physicians "interfere with natural processes" by trying to alter the original design. In the United States, most healthy women continue to give birth in hospitals otherwise designed for treating the sick. This labels them as obstetrics *patients* and helps explain why they are subjected too often to ultrasound, amniocentesis, electronic monitoring devices, and far too often, to surgical procedures.

In most hospitals, when a normal infant is born, the cord is clamped, and as soon as the baby is breathing well, he or she is exhibited to the mother. Usually within a few minutes, the infant is then taken by a nurse to be observed, weighed, measured, superficially examined, given a wrist-band and a footprint for identification and rapidly transported in a warm bassinet to a nursery for close observation and routine laboratory studies. Consequently, the two people who need each other as much as or more than at any other time of their lives are too often abruptly separated. The mother needs the baby as much as the baby needs the mother. The immediate need for close body contact, including suckling at the breast, is only beginning to be recognized. In our culture, breast-feeding, unless done in private, has been considered by many to be somewhat beneath human dignity.

More than a century ago, Dr. William John Little associated a group of spastic deformities with a deficiency of oxygen occurring during difficult and abnormal births. He concluded that virtually nothing other than abnormal births caused the clinical findings he described which we now know to be cerebral palsy. His concept remains entrenched in current textbooks of pediatrics, neonatology, neurology and obstetrics. It has influenced the opinions and practices of many obstetricians and pediatricians and accounts, in part, for the frequent malpractice actions against those who deliver babies and resuscitate them.

There has been increasing evidence in recent years to challenge the long-accepted causation of cerebral palsy. For example, (1) most children with cerebral palsy have no evidence of oxygen deficiency at birth; (2) there is a poor correlation between lack of oxygen and the occurrence of cerebral palsy; (3) the great improvement in perinatal mortality during the past twenty-five years has been accompanied by an essentially unchanged incidence of cerebral palsy (some studies even show an increase); (4) animal studies of oxygen deficiency fail to produce cerebral palsy. Moreover, the high frequency of other birth abnormalities in children with cerebral palsy suggests that brain damage is more likely prenatal and often may be related partly or wholly to early developmental defects.[12]

Our state of knowledge today regarding causes of cerebral palsy is incomplete. Developmental brain damage during fetal development predisposes one to a difficult birth, which may lead to a false impression that the birth itself is responsible for brain damage. It will be interesting to see how this trend may affect future malpractice litigation. The blame may shift from the obstetrician or pediatrician to the one responsible for the health of the mother in early pregnancy.

In conclusion, we believe it is time to reevaluate what is being done in regard to childbirth, even with the best of intentions. For healthy women, labor and birth again need to become a more natural and acceptable experience of life.

Notes

1. C. D. Kimball, "Commentary," *ICEH Review* 4:(3):7, 1980.

2. F. Lamaze, *Painless Childbirth: The Lamaze Method*. Chicago: Regenery, 1970.

3. M. Karmel, *Thank You, Dr. Lamaze*. Philadelphia: J. B. Lippincott, 1959.

4. G. Dick-Read, *Childbirth Without Fear*, pp. 61-62. New York: Harper & Row, 1970.

5. H. Thoms, and E. Karlowski, "Two Thousand Deliveries Under Training for Childbirth Program," *Am. J. Obstet. Gynecol.* 68:279, 1954.

6. J. J. Bonica, *Principles and Practice of Obstetric Analgesia and Anesthesia*, Vols. I and II. Philadelphia: F. A. Davis, 1969.

7. M. Eisenstein, *The Home Court Advantage*. Library of Congress Catalogue No. 88-091225, 1988. Copies available through Homefirst Health Services Offices (312-539-0808).

8. S. Kitzinger, *Giving Birth*. New York: Toplinger, 1971.

9. M., Klaus, and J. Kennell, *Maternal Infant Bonding*. St. Louis: Mosby, 1976.

10. H. Ratner, "The History of the Dehumanization of American Obstetrical Practice," *Child and Family* 16:4–27, 1977.

11. G. White, "Hospital Births," *Child and Family* 20:185–194, 1988. See also note 7, above.

12. J. M. Freeman, (ed.) "Prenatal and Perinatal Foetone Associated with Brain Disorders," *Nat. Institute of Health* No. 85–1149, 1985. K. B. Nelson, et al: "Antecedents of Cerebral Palsy," *New England Journal of Medicine* 315:81, 1986.

Chapter 2

Pregnancy and Nutrition

A full-term healthy human infant is nine months old at birth.

For the nine months of intrauterine life the nutritional requirement of a developing child is a well-nourished mother.

During the nineteenth century, much of what had been recommended about food intake during pregnancy was based on mere experience without the aid of science. At that time, little information was available on the nutrient composition of foods or their biological values. In the early twentieth century, rapid advances in knowledge through the biological sciences gradually made this information available. It was not until the 1940s that the Food and Nutrition Board of the United States National Research Council, our most prestigious national scientific body, appointed a committee to recommend dietary allowances for women during pregnancy.

In 1956, the author, as a member of this Board, as well as a member of the council on Foods and Nutrition of the American Medical Association, held a national conference on Nutrition in Pregnancy at the University of Missouri, Columbia. The objective of the conference was to help inform practicing physicians of advances in this field. Subsequently, a Subcommittee on Maternal Nutrition was appointed by this Food and Nutrition Board to provide a comprehensive review of the knowledge then available and to make practical recommendations for improving the nutritional condition of women before conception and during pregnancy and lactation. After a three-year study, the committee made a report entitled "Maternal Nutrition and the Course of Pregnancy."[1]

Evidence from the committee's report and from subsequent studies has produced a considerable body of knowledge about the importance of the nutritional status of women at the time of conception, as well as on the importance of the kind and amounts of food to be eaten during the various stages of pregnancy. Higher risks were confirmed for women at both ends of the age cycle during pregnancy. The very young teenage mother adds to the nutritional requirements of her own growth the additional needs introduced by her pregnancy. At the other end of the reproductive span, medical hazards and risks increase with age, including the nutritional status and general health of the older mother. The number of pregnancies and the intervals between pregnancies also greatly influence the nutritional status of the mother and the outcome of future pregnancies.

The general health and physical fitness at the time of conception was found to be related closely to the life-long living and eating habits of the women as well as to those of previous generations. Relatively fixed eating habits develop gradually. Recent observations in the United States indicate that older children, especially during adolescence, often develop poor dietary habits (characterized by erratic food intake, consumption of excessive amounts of poor quality, packaged foods and large quantities of sweetened carbonated beverages which contain only limited nutrients).

Accumulated evidence clearly indicates the extent to which nutritional reserves established before conception will greatly influence the course of a woman's pregnancy and the well-being of her baby. After conception there are three biological entities involved: the mother, the placenta and the rapidly developing unborn infant. The nutritional needs of each varies during the course of pregnancy.

I wish to emphasize that *for the nine months of intrauterine life, unborn infants require a well-nourished mother*. Human and animal studies have disclosed that the nutritional status of mothers before and during pregnancy are closely related to maternal and infant illnesses and deaths.[2] Many studies have confirmed that women who are malnourished (underweight or obese) at the time of conception are much more likely to have a spontaneous abortion or to deliver low birth weight or high birth weight infants. Illnesses, deaths and abnormal development are much more common in these under-or overweight infants.[3]

Babies are not born equal with respect to maturity and the composition of their bodies.[4] During the last four weeks of a normal pregnancy, an infant of a healthy mother gains about two pounds. This weight contains nearly one-half of the total protein, calcium and iron of a normal full-term infant's body.[5] The incidence of prematurity has been shown to rise with decreasing maternal nutritional status.[6]

In the United States an ever-increasing number of "poorly-born" (that is premature and postmature) infants are being kept alive in regional medical centers with neonatal intensive care units. To be effective, these intensive care units require a highly-trained health team, expensive and complicated equipment and specialized laboratory resources. Most of these premature infants are denied human milk (especially colostrum and transitional milk) and are fed modified cow's milk. For many reasons, in addition to the nutritional factors, a higher percentage of these "poorly-born" infants who survive, have serious problems in later life.

As was confirmed by the National Research Council study and as observed daily in clinical practice, foods eaten by pregnant women usually do not differ conspicuously, except in quantity, from their lifetime dietary habits, unless the mother is receiving and accepts intensive health guidance and support. The common practice of many doctors of prescribing expensive vitamins and mineral supplements does not meet the protein, caloric and other essential nutrients needed by many pregnant women. In contrast, women in a good nutritional state and with good eating habits require only an increase in the size of their servings in order to satisfy their increased appetite and to ensure a normal weight gain during pregnancy.

Three groups of pregnant women in the United States are especially vulnerable to poor nutritional status: adolescents who are immature and not prepared for the added stress of pregnancy, young women with limited education and economic resources, and older women in suboptimal states of physical fitness, especially those over thirty years of age who have had poor dietary and other health habits. In recent years, these three groups of women are bearing a high percentage of children born in the United States. Young adolescent girls comprise a very vulnerable group, as they are not ready physically or emotionally to assume the substantial responsibilities of motherhood.[7]

We now know that it is physiological (that is, natural) for pregnant women to store additional body fat during pregnancy in preparation for lactation and for the increased energy needed to care for a baby, and to gradually re-establish normal body weight during lactation. Consequently, women who did not nurse their infants and had closely-spaced pregnancies were prone to become obese. As a result, in the mid-part of this century, most doctors were taught to monitor weight gain closely and to encourage women to restrict food intake during pregnancy, and, as a safeguard, to take various relatively expensive nutritional supplements. Unfortunately, far too little attention was directed to devising meal plans in keeping with the food habits of the mothers, so as to ensure the intake of essential nutrients and to help modify faulty food habits. There are now reliable data which indicate that a weight gain of about 27 pounds during pregnancy is desirable and produces the most favorable results. For underweight women, the optimal weight gain has been found to be over 30 pounds. These observations also confirmed that excessive weight gain during pregnancy is undesirable. Meals should be planned to include all of the essential nutrients required to support the normal development and growth of the unborn child without depleting the mother's nutritional stores. The studies also indicate that even those mothers who are grossly overweight (obese) should improve their dietary habits and gain about 20 pounds during pregnancy.[8]

As a result of this ever-increasing body of knowledge derived from basic and clinical research studies, practices for enhancing the nutritional state of women are evolving. Earlier misplaced priorities such as strict weight control, unnecessary vitamin and mineral supplements and salt restriction should now be replaced with practical instructions on the preparation of simple meals to meet the known nutritional requirements for the various stages of pregnancy. Experience indicates that this is best done by individual assessment and by altering faulty eating habits through counseling by a trained health team. A broader application of the "team" concept would help to bridge the provider-consumer gap that still exists in many communities.

In most communities in Western societies, there are readily available simple meal plans, in keeping with cultural and ethnic habits, for attaining and maintaining good nutrition, before and during pregnancy. However, I would like to enumerate some facts and practices which have been found helpful for improving the eating habits of many families.

1) Establish regular times for eating meals and snacks each day.
2) Have about the same amount of high quality foods in each of the three regular meals. This usually means eating a larger breakfast and a smaller evening meal.
3) Avoid foods and drinks containing large amounts of simple sugar (i.e., candy, frostings and other foods such as carbonated drinks).
4) Use high-quality, common seasonal foods on a daily basis to prepare simple meals.
5) Include a protein source in each meal. Milk, whole grain cereals and bread, meat, fish, poultry and eggs are foods rich in protein.
6) Include one or possibly two eggs daily in meals. (Eggs are nature's way of packaging essential nutrients, including iron and trace elements, especially needed by pregnant and lactating mothers, as well as by rapidly growing young children and adolescents. Remember, when a hen sits on a fertilized egg for three weeks, a chick, with all of its diverse anatomical parts, develops).
7) Use the somewhat more expensive margarines rather than

cheaper heat-treated margarine or butter. Natural vegetable and fish oils are more nutritious than heat-treated vegetable oils or animal fats. Limit the intake of animal fats and cream.

8) Provide vitamins and minerals by eating a wide variety of wholesome foods, such as fruits and vegetables, whole grain breads and cereals, eggs, vitamin-fortified milk and meats or legumes (such as beans or peas). Vitamin supplements (pills) are relatively expensive and are not needed by healthy people who are eating well-planned meals. Too many vitamins especially A, D, E and K, can also be harmful.

9) Discourage the use of low-calorie "dietetic" sweets, except for an occasional social situation. Cultivating and perpetuating a "sweet tooth" and substituting empty calories for sound nutrition is undesirable not only during pregnancy but also in daily family life. Children's eating habits are developed primarily by the example of their parents, siblings, and close friends.

The importance and scientific basis of applied nutrition is being taught quite effectively in most quality secondary schools and high schools in Western societies. However, as indicated, the practical application of this knowledge leaves much to be desired. A comprehensive review of the facts about natural health and simple, practical directives for applying this knowledge should be included in the instructions for couples preparing for marriage. Couples need to appreciate the importance of the woman's being in an optimal state of health prior to conception, her need to avoid exposure to infections, smoking and alcohol, especially during the first eight weeks of pregnancy when the baby is in the critical period of rapid development.[9]

Although for many women it is very difficult to stop smoking, a concerted effort in this regard should be made well before marriage. There are extensive data to indicate the adverse effect that smoking has on female and male fertility, early and late pregnancy outcomes, infant birthweights and even the future health of children.[10]

There also are extensive scientific data to indicate a positive correlation between maternal alcohol consumption and fetal abnormalities, including fetal alcohol syndrome, which consists of: (1) pre-or post-birth growth retardation; (2) developmental delay or intellectual impairment; (3) small head size and poorly developed facial features.[11] Before and during pregnancy women should restrict the use of alcoholic drinks to no more than a small glass of wine or beer at the noon or evening meal.

In addition to the very serious problem pertaining to the use of narcotic drugs, American women who are currently of reproductive age have been raised in a serious but less appreciated and dramatic drug culture. They have been exposed to daily radio and television messages that infer that all symptoms requre medication. Therefore, it is difficult to modify a woman's behavior during pregnancy when fairly frequent minor symptoms may occur. Preconception counseling concerning all manner of drug use should begin early and reach all women from puberty to menopause. In recent years such an approach has resulted in considerable success with regard to a decrease in fetal exposure to caffeine, nicotine and alcohol.

Notes

1. *Maternal Nutrition and the Course of Pregnancy*. Committee on Maternal Nutrition. Food and Nutrition Board, National Research Council National Academy of Sciences, Washington, DC, 1970.

2. *Nutrition in Pregnancy and Lactation*. WHO Tech. Rep. Ser. No. 302. World Health Organization, Geneva, 1965.

3. W. T. Tompkins, et al., "Maternal and Newborn Studies at Philadelphia Lying-in Hospital," *Promotion of Maternal and Newborn Health*, Milbank Memorial Fund, New York, 1955.

4. B. M. Kagan, V. Stanicova, N. S. Felix, J. Hodgman, and D. Kalman, "Body Composition of Premature Infants: Relation to Nutrition," *American Journal of Clinical Nutrition* 25: 1153–64, 1972.

5. T. Schulman, "Iron Requirements in Infancy," *JAMA* 175118,1961.

6. P. C. Jean, M. Smith, and G. Stearns, "Dietary Habits of Pregnant Women of Low Income in Iowa," *Journal of the American Diet. Assn.* 31:576, 1955.

7. *Maternal Nutrition and the Course of Pregancy*, see footnote 1, above.

8. Committee on Maternal Nutrition, Food & Nutrition Board, National Academy of Sciences, National Research Council, Washington, D.C., pp. 133/977.

9. B.S. Worthing, and J. Vermeerck, *Nutrition in Pregnancy and Lactation*. St. Louis: Mosby, 1981.

10. P. V. Cole, L. H. Hawkins, and D. Roberts, "Smoking During Pregnancy and its Effects on the Fetus, *Journal of Obstetrics and Gynecology of the British Commonwealth* 79:782, 1972.

11. J. W. Hanson, R. L. Streissguth, and D. W. Smith, "The Effects of Moderate Alcohol Consumption During Pregnancy on Fetal Growth and Morphogenesis," *Journal of Pediatrics* 92: 457, 1978. K. L. Jones, et al. "Patterns of Malformation in Offspring of Chronic Alcoholic Mothers," *Lancet* 1:1267, 1973.

Chapter 3

Ecological Breast-Feeding

Human milk from well-nourished mothers meets all of the nutritional needs of their "well-born" babies, including vitamin D, from the time of birth until about the sixth month of postnatal life. In addition, human milk, especially colostrum and early transitional milk, contains many anti-infective substances which decrease both the incidence and the severity of infections during infancy.[1]

Until early in the twentieth century, breast (natural) feeding was essential for infant survival. The only alternative for mothers unwilling or unable to nurse their infants was a "wet nurse". Attempts at artificial feeding almost uniformly led to early death for the infant.

Ecological or biological breastfeeding consists of: (1) feeding only human milk for about six months; (2) suckling on demand day and night (after about two months most full-term breast-fed infants sleep from the late evening feeding until the early morning feeding, a period of five to six hours); (3) no pacifiers; (4) gradual introduction of small amounts of selected foods at about six months; and (5) continuation of nursing as the primary source of food for about one year or a little longer.

Major advances in artificial feeding did not occur until the second and third decades of the present century. Success in artificial feeding gradually became possible due to the proliferation of techniques based on new knowledge in many areas, including simple methods for modifying cow's milk, development of sanitary methods for handling, refrigerating and distributing cow's milk, and the development of improved rubber nipples and nursing bottles. Of crucial importance was recognition of the need for and availability of vitamin supplementation. There were also rapid advances in technology and commercial availability of various modified cow's milk formulas.

In the first decade of the twentieth century, pasteurization of cow's milk was introduced and the relationship between intestinal bacteria and infantile diarrhea was recognized; scurvy was found to be a specific nutritional deficiency disease. However, vitamin C, the vitamin needed to prevent scurvy was not identified as ascorbic acid until 1931. In the second decade, cod liver oil was shown to prevent rickets and various vitamin-fortified, evaporated-milk preparations became commercially available. In the 1920s and 1930s, it first became known that the active substance in cod liver oil is a fat-soluble substance called vitamin D. Vitamin D was not prepared in pure form until 1931. Homogenization, which ensured the even despersal of vitamin D throughout the milk, only became widespread in 1940.

As improved cow's milk preparations became commercially available and were tolerated by most infants, many doctors, nurses and parents gradually came to accept that cow's milk formulas were just about as good as human milk for feeding infants. As a result, the incidence of natural feeding of newborn infants in the United States decreased from 60 percent in the 1940s to less than 30 percent in 1950. In 1958, the frequency of breast-feeding at one month had declined to about 20 percent and had further decreased to less than 10 percent by the age of four months. A study in 1966 indicated that at six months, less than 5 percent of infants in the United States were being breast-fed and most also had been receiving other foods by two to four months of age.[2] The rapidity of change from natural (breast) to artificial (bottle) feeding clearly indicates that the transition came about as a result of psychological and sociological factors, rather than from physiological causes. Human lactation is highly influenced by a wide variety of interrelated factors, including individual emotions and attitudes as well as group-derived attitudes.

Until about 1920, solid foods were seldom offered to infants before one year of age. By 1937, most pediatricians favored introduction of solid foods by two to four months of age in order to meet the nutritional needs, especially iron, of infants fed by formula (i.e., artificially). The 1966 study reported that many mothers were already feeding cereals and strained foods to both breast-and bottle-fed babies by one to two months of age, and surprisingly, most of the infants tolerated them quite well.[3]

Many of the differences that exist in the composition of human and cow's milk were well-known even in the late nineteenth century. In fact, the modification and consequent tolerance of cow's milk formulas was based on how well they emulated characteristics of human milk. With improved cow's milk preparations containing vitamin and mineral supplements, babies seemed to thrive and, as previously stated, many health providers and parents adopted the attitude that cow's milk formulas were just about as good as human milk for feeding infants. Nevertheless, we have continued to learn that the differences in the milks from one species to another are much more diverse and subtle than had previously been known or even suspected.

Infants continue to grow very rapidly during the early months of postnatal life. It is important to meet the needs of infants fully and continuously during this period of very rapid growth and development. Nutritional imbalance during these early postnatal months has lasting effects not only on physical growth and development, but also on the emotional and intellectual development of the child.

During pregnancy and lactation there is a biologic continuum which allows for the transfer of nutrients, protective substances and growth modulators from mother to baby. During the entire period of infancy (about 12 months), many important biological adaptations occur, especially in the infants's digestive tract and the immune system, changes which greatly effect the infant's health and growth.[4]

The composition of human milk from a well-nourished mother changes daily (especially during the critical early months of postnatal life) in order to provide all the essential nutrients in proper balance. Also, the milk suckled from the breast actually becomes richer, that is, it has a higher fat content during nursing and automatically develops an appetite control mechanism. This aids in the prevention of obesity, which is the most common and serious nutritional problem in our society.[5] Evidence is accumulating that adult-onset diabetes results from long-term obesity and that the duration of obesity is probably more important than the degree of obesity in determining which fat individuals will develop diabetes.[6] Infants of diabetic mothers, (whether it be the mild form of diabetes which develops during pregnancy or the uncontrolled more severe forms requiring insulin), become markedly obese *in utero*. Many artificially-fed infants also become obese, partly because they ingest excessive amounts of formula as a result of being overfed from bottles with too free-flowing nipples.

Fat in human milk is a major energy source for the newborn infant. The content and composition of human milk fat changes rapidly during early lactation, meeting the special needs of newborn infants. Essential fatty acid levels are much higher in colostrum and transitional milk and have been found to be important for the optimal growth of the rapidly developing nervous system.[7]

The amount of cholesterol in human milk is higher than the amount in cow's milk and even more so than that found in most commercial cow's milk formulas, which are often made with various vegetable oils containing little or no cholesterol. From animal experiments, it has been found that relatively high intakes of cholesterol are needed in early life to insure the development of appropriate special substances called enzymes that are needed in later life to control the blood cholesterol levels.[8] It has also been recognized that a high cholesterol diet is necessary to promote peripheral nerve myelin and brain white matter development during the critical stage of rapid brain growth in early infancy.

The zinc and copper ratio in human milk also is much lower than the amount found in cow's milk, and recent studies suggest that the ingestion of a proper balance of these minerals also may be a factor in preventing heart disease later in life.[9] Indeed, there is considerable evidence that the blood vessel changes that ultimately cause coronary heart disease begin in the early years of life and that preventive measures, to be more effective, must be instituted during pregnancy, infancy or early childhood. The observation of pathological (abnormal) changes in the large blood vessels of some young children suggests that the nutritional status of the infant at birth and the type of feeding in early life may be contributing to the increasing problems of coronary heart disease in adult life.[10]

Mechanical differences in bottle-feeding and breast-feeding are very considerable and may lead to malocclusion, that is, malalignment of the teeth. In bottle feeding, the main action is sucking, which causes a negative pressure and consequently increases the use of large-holed nipples which require less sucking. Breast-feeding is a process of "suckling", in which negative pressure suction plays only a minor role. When the baby sucks, the milk is expressed from the breast by the "milking action" of the tongue moving and squeezing the nipple against the hard palate, and also by the active flow of the milk from the breast due to the maternal letdown reflex. A special form of tooth decay of the upper front teeth, has been termed "nursing bottle syndrome", and occurs only in bottle-fed infants, especially those given propped bottles.[11] The sweetness of many formula feedings also may condition the child to desire sweetened foods, which carries the added potential of tooth decay and an increased tendency to obesity, two major nutritional dietary public health problems in Western societies.[12] Moreover, malalignment of the teeth (shown to result from lack of breast-feeding) in itself is associated with an increased rate of tooth decay and often requires distressful and expensive orthodontic treatment.[13]

Intolerance to feeding pasteurized homogenized cow's milk in early infancy without additional heating was found to cause an intestinal disorder resulting in continuous small losses of blood and protein in the stools.[14] The blood loss gradually resulted in iron-deficiency anemia, which in the 1950s became one of the most common and serious illnesses of infants fed unmodified, pasteurized, homogenized milk. Present thinking would relate this hypersensitivity primarily to the maturity of the infant. However, the finding of similar problems in quite a few older children and adults would suggest that recovery, although it occurs in the majority of infants, does not always take place and that continued or recurrent intolerance to cow's milk protein does persist into adult life.[15]

Allergic disorders have increased in our industrialized societies and occur in response to a wide range of different allergens, including foods. In infants and young children, the most common food allergies are to cow's milk proteins, wheat, and other protein-containing foods that are fed too early to young infants.[16]

With improved laboratory methods for analysis of both human milk and cow's milk, it gradually became more and more obvious that cow's milk is tailored for calves and human milk is tailored for infants. Analysis also indicates that the composition of human milk undergoes rapid daily changes during the early days and weeks of the postpartum period to coincide with the special nutritional and immunological (disease-preventing) needs of the newborn infant during the critical transition period to life outside the womb. Consequently, given our new knowledge, many medical articles began to appear in the world literature in the middle of this century confirming the superiority of natural versus artificial feeding of infants.[17] However, it was not until 1974 that a resolution was adopted by the World Health Organization urging all member countries to undertake vigorous action to stress the importance of breast-feeding, and it was not until 1978 that the Committee on Nutrition of the American Academy of Pediatrics and the Nutrition Committee of the Canadian Pediatric Society prepared a joint statement in support of breast-feeding.[18]

In 1985, a special issue on infant feeding was published in the pediatric literature detailing many additional diverse and subtle differences between human mild and modified cow's milk formulas. [19] A few examples will suffice to indicate the recent rapid extension of our knowledge in this regard. In human milk, lactalbumin is the principal protein, while in cow's milk, casein is the principal protein. Each has markedly different internal structures. The concentration and compositions of other proteins in human and cow's milk are now known to be very different. In human milk, the proteins have been found to contain highly specialized components which protect the infant from infections. More recently, other protein substances have been identified, including growth modulators and hormones. Lactoferrin, a milk-specific, iron-binding protein, has been identifed and found to be present in moderate concentrations in human milk, and only in trace amounts in cow's milk. Lactoferrin plays an important role in the process of iron absorption in the intestine and, in addition, helps control infections. Lactoferrin protects breast-fed infants from developing iron deficiency anemia, a serious clinical problem in bottle-fed babies.[20] Substances called lysozymes have also been identifed in moderate concentrations in human milk, but only in trace amounts in cow's milk. These lysozymes act as anti-bacterial agents in the intestinal tract to prevent and control infections. [21]

Fortunately, in its own proper way, nature provides a means of protecting the newborn infant against the vulnerability of the immature intestinal defense system: the first milk (colostrum) and the early transitional human milk, contains not only antibodies, but also live white blood cells and other substances that prevent bacterial growth and damage to the tissues. For this reason, all mothers should be encouraged to nurse their newborn infants for at least the first few weeks of postnatal life—even if they have to be separated from their babies to work outside thier home soon after delivery. Colostrum is actually a live tissue specially designed for the transition of the infant from intrauterine to extrauterine life, and to protect the baby from infections.[22]

Scientific data on which to base sound nutritional advice during late infancy is more limited. What is well documented is that the weaning process is naturally a lengthy one (a matter of months, not days or weeks) and that the gradual introduction of selected foods need not inhibit a mother's ability to lactate and continue to supply the major source of high quality protein and other essential nutrients and calories for her baby.[23] How long breast-feeding should be continued depends on many factors, sociological and economic as well as physiological and psychological, of which the needs of the infant are a major consideration. There are good arguments for extending breast-feeding at least through the first year or more of postnatal life.[24] Unquestionably, extensive scientific data also confirms that other selected foods are necessary for optimal infant nutrition, from the second half-year of postnatal life.

In the recent past, most mothers in Western countries were advised by doctors and nurses to breast-feed their infants only five to seven times a day, and when the baby demanded more food than she could apparently supply, to offer supplementary bottle feeding. Ironically, however, since the suckling actually stimulates milk production, if the mother followed this advice, her milk output immediately decreased—and additional supplementary feedings then became necessary. So breast-feeding was gradually replaced by bottle-feeding over a period of a few short weeks or months. This very common type of breast-feeding is not ecological.

Notes

1. A. S. Cunningham, "Morbidity in Breast-fed and Artificially-fed Infants," *J. Pediat.* 90: 726–9, 1977. J. W. Gerrard, "Breast-feeding: Second Thoughts," *Pediatrics* 54:757–64, 1974. Reprinted in *Child and Family* 16: 114, 1977. S. Goldman and C. W. Smith, "Host Resistance Factors in Human Milk." *J. Pediat.* 82: 1082–90, 1973. P. Gyorgy, "Human Milk Differences," First Wyeth Nutrition Symposium. Wyeth Laboratories, Philadephia, 1973, pp. 1–7. L. A. Hasson, et al. "Immune Defense Factors in Human Milk," *Mod. Probll. Paedit.* 15: 63, 1975. A. M. Larguine, et al. "Immunidad local en el recien nacido. Primera experiencia con la administracion de calostro homano a recien nacidos preterimino," *Arch. Argent. Paedit.* 72: 169, 1974. S. A. Larsen, and D. R. Homer, "Relation of Breast-versus Bottle-feeding to Hospitalization for Gastroenterities in a Middle Class U.S. Population," *J. Pediat.* 92: 417–8, 1978. J. Pitt, et al. "Macrophages and the Protective Action of Breast Milk in Necrotizing Enterocolitis," *Pediatr. Res.* 8: 384, 1974.

2. E. J. Saber, and M. Feinlieb, "Breast-feeding," *Pediatrics* 37: 299, 1966.

3. L. A., Hanson, et al. "Protective Factors in Milk and the Development of the Immune System," *Pediatrics* 75 (Supp.): 172–176, 1985.

4. See preceding note.

5. B. Hall, "Changing Composition of Human Milk and Early Development of an Appetite Control," *Lancet* 1: 779–81, 1975. M. Ounsted, and G. Sleigh, "The Infant's Self-Regulation of Food Intake and Weight Gain Difference in Metabolic Balance after Growth Constraint or Acceleration *in utero*," *Lancet* 1:1393–7, 1975.

6. P. Asher, "Fat Babies and Fat Children: Prognosis of Obesity in the Very Young," *Arch. Dis. Child.* 41: 672, 1966. R. L. Jackson, "Relationship of Obesity to Diabetes," *Missouri Med.* 73: 221–6, 1976.

7. R. Vany, M. Treen, and D. Hoffman, "Essential Fatty Acid Metabolism and Requirements during Development," *Seminars in Perinatology* 13: 2, 1989, pp. 118–130. Watkins, J. B. "Lipid Digestion and Absorption," *Pediatrics* 75 (Supp.): 151–156, 1985. M. Winick, J. A. Brasel, and P. Rosso, "Nutrition and Cell Growth," in M. Winick (ed.) *Current Concepts in Nutrition. Vol. 1: Nutrition and Development.* New York: John Wiley and Sons, Inc., 1972.

8. R. Reiser, and Z. Sidelman, "Control of Serum Cholesterol Homeostasis by Cholesterol in the Milk of the Suckling Rat, : *J. Nutr.* 102: 1009–16, 1972.

9. C. D. Eckherdt, et al. "Zinc Binding: A Difference between Human and Bovine Milk," *Science,* 1975: 789–790, 1977. L. M. Klevay, "The Ratio of Zinc to Copper in Milk and Mortality Due to Coronary Artery Disease. An Association," in D. D. Hemphill (ed.) *Trace Substance in Environmental Health VIII.* Columbia: University of Missouri, 1974.

10. S. C. Mitchell, "Symposium on Prevention of Atherosclerosis at the Pediatric Level, Including Identification of Potential Risks and Prophyaxis," *Amer. J. Cardiol.* 31: 539–41, 1973.

11. A. L. Golnick, and R. J. Mathewson, "Nursing Bottle Syndrome: More Can Be Done," *J. Mich. State Dent. Assn.* 49–261, 1967.

12. G. B. Winter, et al. "The Prevalence of Dental Caries in Preschool Children Aged 1–4," *Brit. Dent. Journal* 130: 434–6, 1971.

13. T. M. Graber, *Etiology of Malocclusion in Orthodontics, Principles and Practice.* Philadelphia: Saunders, 1966 (see ch. 6).

14. P. Kuitenen, et al. "Responses of the Jejunal Mucosa to Cow's Milk in the Malabsorbtion Syndrome with Cow's Milk Intolerance," *Acta Paedit. Scand.* 62: 585–95, 1973. J. A. McMillan, S. A. Landau, and

F. A. Oski, "Iron Sufficiency in Breast-fed Infants and the Availability of Iron from Human Milk," *Pediatrics* 58: 686–91, 1976.

15. C. W. Woodruff, "Milk Intolerance," *Nutr. Res.* 34: 33–7, 1976.

16. J. W. Gerrard, "Allergy in Infancy," *Pediat. Ann.* 3: 9, 1974. A. S. Goldman, "Cow Milk Sensitivity: A Review." *Swedish Nutritional Foundation Symposium on Food and Immunology.* Stockholm: Almquist and Wiskell, 1977. S. R. Halpren, et al. "Development of Childhood Allergy in Infants Fed Breast, Soy and Cow's Milk," *J. Allergy Clin. Immunol.* 51: 139–51, 1973.

17. J. W. Gerrard, see footnote 1, above. R. L. Jackson, "Long-term Consequences of Suboptimal Nutrition in Early Life," *Pediatric Clinics of North America* 24: 63–69, 1977. D. B. Jelliffe, and E. E. P. Jelliffe, "The Uniqueness of Human Milk," *Amer., J. Lin. Nutr.* 24: 968–1024, 1971.

18. "Commentary: Breast-feeding," *Amer. Acad. Pub. Comm. on Nutrition* 57: 270–85, 1976.

19. "Current Issues in Feeding the Normal Infant," *Pediatrics* 85 (Supp.): 135–215, 1985.

20. G. B. Fransson, "The Role of Lactoferrin in Iron Absorption and its Relation to Nutritional Status," in Kaufmann, W. (ed.), *Role of Milk Proteins in Human Nutrition.* Gelsen Kirchen-Buer, Verlag Th. Mann, 1983, pp. 441–443.

21. A. Bezkorovainy, "Human Milk and Colostrum Proteins: A Review," *J. Dairy Sci.* 60: 1023, 1977. L. Hambreus, "The Physiological Significance of Human Milk Proteins," *Nordic Research Seminar*, Oregound, Sweden, 1984. 22. See footnote 3, above.

23. R. G. Whitehead, "The Human Weaning Process," *Pediatrics* 75 (Supp.) 189–193, 1985.

24. L. Waletzky, "Weaning from the Breast," *Child and Family* 17: 166–176, 1978.

Chapter 4

Psychology and Endocrinology of Breast-feeding

Breast-feeding is not only a means of supplying nutrients to the baby, but also automatically provides an intimate interrelationship (bonding) between the mother and her baby. Endocrinological alterations (that is, changing levels of hormones in the body) result in natural changes in post-partum mothers that lead to bonding with their infants.[1] After a natural delivery, a healthy newborn baby is very alert and responsive. Recent studies indicate that for optimal mothering, the baby should have immediate body contact with the mother after birth, and nursing should occur as soon as possible. During pregnancy, the placental hormones estrogen and progesterone inhibit milk production (this is why giving these hormones in birth control pills is contraindicated during lactation).

Oxytocin, a pituitary hormone, stimulates uterine contractions during labor. It also has another important function in initiating and maintaining lactation. After birth, oxytocin secretion is produced by various sensory stimuli such as hearing the baby's cry, cuddling the baby, and by the baby rooting for the nipple. Oxytocin acts on specialized cells in the breast to eject or "let down" the milk. The natural release of oxytocin precedes suckling. Before suckling, most newborn infants stimulate the nipple by licking or nuzzling it. Some newborn infants are reluctant to suck until the nipple is erect and ejecting fluid.[2] It is for these reasons that newborn infants need to remain in close contact with their mothers. It is unnatural to have a healthy newborn infant separated from its mother and brought to her for nursing only during short scheduled time periods. When mothers are able to respond to nature, they increase the enjoyment they will have from a closer, life-long love affair with their children and their grandchildren. Until recently, the bonding and sensuous enjoyment derived from breast-feeding were poorly appreciated by Western society.

Dr. Herbert Ratner recently wrote an excellent series of editorials on "The Nursing Couplet."[3] The final one, on "The Mother's Face," analyses how the intimate interrelationship between the nursing mother and her infant affects the child's early development. In this classic presentation from art and literature, the author depicts how the warm embracing acceptance given by a nursing mother to her newborn infant in the first hours, days and weeks after birth, plays a large role in determining how the young infant will view the world and others about him or her.

All aspects of infant feeding have subtle psychological implications and consequences. With a long-lived species such as man, with so many variables between families within each culture, and with changes in society occurring rapidly and continually, it is impossible to identify and enumerate all aspects of the mother-baby interaction and to evaluate their relative influences objectively. It is obvious that not all breast-fed babies grow up to be healthy and well-adjusted or that all bottle-fed babies grow up to be poorly developed or maladjusted. It is always obvious, however, that nature's method of feeding ensures the optimum intimate, loving interrelationship of mother and infant.

In advising breast-feeding, great care must be taken not to stress its importance to such a degree that a mother who is unable to continue to nurse her infant will feel inadequate or blameworthy. In recent years we have extended our knowledge of the nutritional requirements of infants and children, and we are continuing to learn how to more effectively feed those infants who are denied human milk. However, all of the evidence indicates that artificial feeding should be used only where the informed mother refuses to nurse her infant, or after an honest attempt at breast-feeding has failed.

Only in recent years have we begun to perceive and understand the economic and social benefits of human milk. This lack of appreciation is not surprising. Human milk has not been considered or classified as a food by agronomists, since it is not grown agriculturally, advertised, or sold for profit. Most food composition tables have not even included human milk. In fact, until now, food balance sheets, which indicate a country's food production, have given little or no attention to the significance of human milk.

As we have stated, in addition to the importance of infant feeding in relation to the proper supply of nutrients, the *ecological* context of breast-feeding is also vital for the prevention of infections and child-spacing. In particular, breast-feeding insures close contact between mother and baby while bottle-feeding encourages the use of substitute caregiving. The future health, nutrition, and emotional development of children in our ever more complex society depends upon the quality of care and attention received by infants. Too often nowadays infants are left at home or taken to homes with untrained baby sitters, or to poorly-staffed and-equipped day care centers. It is well established that infant and preschool children who were cared for by their own mothers during these early critical years of life have fewer problems of growth and development. The emotional and intellectual development of children occurs at the fastest rate during infancy and the early preschool years, and it is very difficult to modify patterns of behavior once the child has attained school age.

Since the first quarter of the present century, artificial feeding has become so simple and apparently successful that the many long-term advantages of natural feeding are even now poorly appreciated. In our science-dominated era, the cultural appeal for doctors, nurses, and dietitians to prescribe a modified, fortified cow's milk formula is easily understood. Consequently, the science and art of breast-feeding is most often taught ineffectively in medical and nursing schools, as well as in departments of home economics. Until recently, textbooks of the various health professions, have contained only minimal references to the anatomy and psychophysiology of breast-feeding. Consequently, those who should be most knowledgeable about the subject are often ill-prepared by education or experience to advise and educate parents in this regard. Physicians, nurses, dietitians, and other allied health professionals have the responsibility to learn the facts not only about the nutritive superiority of human milk, but also about the long-term health hazards of bottle-feeding.

Many influences have crept into modern living to dissuade mothers from breast-feeding. An ever-increasing number of mothers are working outside the home. Many mothers accept the common practice of artificial feeding as more convenient and better adapted to their way of living; most do not understand and have not had the advantages of breast-feeding explained to them.

Between 1971 and 1978, the prevalence of breast-feeding increased substantially for all infant ages surveyed. During this period, breast-feeding in hospitals almost doubled, rising from 25% to 47%; in particular, the rate of increase was as follows: at two months, from 14% to 35%; at 3–5 months, from 8% to 27%; and by 5–6 months, from 6% to 21%. The highest increase occurred among mothers with at least some college education. The survey showed that not only were more mothers breast-feeding, but also they were continuing to nurse for longer periods of time. The increased incidence was greater for, but was not limited to higher income and better educated mothers. Overall, (that is, in hospitals and away from them) the practice of breast-feeding almost tripled, even among mothers whose education did not extend beyond elementary or high school and among those attending public clinics.[4]

A recent report (1985)[5] has documented a moderate increase in both the incidence and the duration of breast-feeding from 1971 to 1982, but both of these gains have since plateaued. The major increase in breast-feeding (37%) occurred in hospitals, indicating improved prenatal education and modifications in hospital practices. A few more mothers with college educations and higher family incomes were found to be nursing and to be doing so for somewhat longer periods of time. However, only a limited number were nursing for more than six months. The relative number of black mothers nursing their babies also increased slightly (3.5%). Mothers who were less than twenty years of age and from socioeconomically depressed families continued to have the lowest incidence, and most of these mothers never nursed.

The cultural rebirth of breast-feeding actually began in 1956, with the formation of the La Leche League. This organization was conceived when two mature young mothers met at a picnic and began talking about their babies. Both of them were nursing a baby at the time, and were concerned about the lack of practical information available about natural feeding (little had been given them). They found it so helpful to discuss their experiences with and concerns about breast-feeding that they decided to meet again soon and to invite other nursing mothers. At their next meeting, there were thirty mothers eager to share their experiences and to learn more about breast-feeding. They discovered how supportive and encouraging it was to meet and share information with each other. Seven nursing mothers from this original group became the founding mothers of the organization, which they decided to name La Leche League. Their inspiration for this name came from the fact that when, in 1620, the early Spanish settlers dedicated the first American Marian Shrine in St. Augustine, Florida, they called it the La Leche Shrine, as Mary is depicted there as a nursing mother.

From this very simple grass-roots beginning, the now international La Leche League had its origin. The objectives of the organization were to provide mother-to-mother support and information about infant care, especially breast-feeding, through monthly local neighborhood discussion meetings, and to collect additional reliable information through study and consultation with health experts in order to communicate this growing body of knowledge to other mothers.[6] By 1988 there were over 4,000 local groups distributed around the world in 43 countries, with about 9,000 accredited discussion leaders. The La Leche League has become the major scientific center for the collection and distribution of breast-feeding and child-rearing information. Last year, over 3 million pieces of information were dispensed in 23 different languages. The author of this book has been and is a member of the medical advisory board of the La Leche League. In recent years, the League has also sponsored an annual accredited scientific conference for physicians and other health workers.

Without doubt, human milk is the safest, least allergenic, most economical, and most readily available source of ideal animal protein for human infants. In addition to wanting to nurse their infants, mothers need the active support and encouragement of their husbands and doctors. More often than they realize, doctors and nurses advocate artificial feeding by the advice they give. In general, supplementary bottle feedings and other baby foods are recommended too early, and in excessive amounts, in order to decrease the frequency of nursing, especially night feedings. In areas of the world where bottle-feeding is common, solid foods are customarily introduced too early and in excessive amounts, whereas in areas of the world where breast-feeding is common, solid foods (which are often of questionable quality) are fed too late and in insufficient amounts.

Our youth are dependent on health professionals to teach them the grave import of their decisions about whether to feed their infants naturally or artifically. For the first year of postnatal life, the feeding of human milk is important not only for the future health of the infant and mother, but also for the stability of the family and the positive or negative influence that each family unit has on society. Parents cannot learn too soon that they must "give of themselves" to provide optimal growth and development of their children.

The physiological and psychological advantages of ecological breast-feeding may be summarized as follows:

1. Through a natural bonding process, breast-feeding reinforces mothers' and babies' love for each other.
2. The hormone prolactin is secreted promptly in the mother in response to nipple stimulation by the child. This calms the mother and automatically suppresses ovulation.
3. Milk from a healthy mother meets *all* of the nutritional needs of a full-term newborn infant for about the first six months of life.
4. The composition of human milk changes daily (especially during the early critical first months after birth) to meet the rapidly changing needs of a young infant. This is equivalent to having a new formula specially prepared for the baby every day.
5. Nursing not only satisfies the baby's appetite, but this close physical contact with the mother also keeps the baby pacified.

Sensuous contact with the baby through nursing also makes the mother more calm and "motherly."

6. Human milk protects babies from many infections. The first milk (colostrum) and early transitional milk contains many anti-infective substances which decrease not only the incidence but also the severity of infections.

7. Breast-fed babies have fewer allergies. Human milk protects against sensitization to cow's milk and other foods needed by young infants who are bottle-fed.

8. Breast-fed babies are much less likely to spit up, vomit or have diarrhea and are never constipated.

9. Breast-fed babies actually smell better because: (a) they are less likely to regurgitate human milk, which in any event doesn't smell sour and offensive as does cow's milk; (b) the stools of breast-fed infants are not putrid as are the stools of bottle-fed babies; and (c) diapers do not smell like ammonia and cause diaper rash.

10. Babies breast-fed "on demand" are usually content and much less likely to have colic in the early months, and in my experience, are less likely to have emotional problems related to eating and sleeping as they grow older.

11. Human milk is always "ready" and needs no refrigeration or preparation.

12. Nursing requires only that the mother drink more fluids and eat slightly higher-quality food; this is *much* less expensive than buying expensive formulas, bottles, and nipples.

13. Breast-fed infants have fewer dental problems in later life: i.e. less dental caries and malocclusions.

14. Ecological breast-feeding automatically suppresses ovulation. Doctors now understand why this happens. In contrast, "token" or partial breast-feeding, customary in many cultures, has, as many are aware, few anovulatory effects, and therefore limited and unreliable spacing effects. If the mother's milk supplies the only food for her baby during the first five to six months and if she continues to nurse at frequent intervals as the baby begins to be given only small feedings of selected high-quality foods during the second half of the first year, she

is very unlikely to begin menstruating and ovulating again until about 9 to 18 months postpartum, depending on how often the baby suckles and how much milk the mother continues to produce. Natural spacing is the topic for the next chapter.

Notes

1. H. S. McNeilly, et al. "Release of Oxytocin and Prolactin in Response to Suckling," *British Med. Journal* 286:257–259, 1983.

2. H. S. McNeilly, et al. "Fertility after Childbirth: Adqeuacy of post-partum luteal phases, *Clinical Endocrinology* 17, 609–615, 1982. R. V. Short, "Lactation: The Central Control of Reproduction," in *Breastfeeding and the Mother*, CIBA Foundation Symposium 45, pp. 73–80, Elsevier, Amsterdam, 1976.

3. H. Ratner, "The Nursing Couplet," Child and Family Reprint Booklet Series, Box 508, Oak Park, IL 60303. A series of editorials on the nursing couplet from *Child and Family* 18:242–243; 19:1–3, 82–83, 162–164, 242–244; 29:3–11, "Introduction, Prelude, Roots, Connaturality, Fidelity, and The Mother's Face."

4. G. A. Martinez and J. P. Nalezienski, "The Recent Trend in Breast-feeding," *Pediatrics* 64:686–690, 1979.

5. G. A. Martinez and F. Krieger, "Milk Feeding Patterns in the United States," *Pediatrics* 76: 1004–1008, 1985.

6. *The Womanly Art of Breast-feeding*. La Leche League International. Franklin Park, IL. Second edition, 1988.

Chapter 5

Natural Spacing

The rapid decline in ecological breast-feeding from 1930 to 1960 resulted in early postpartum ovulation and an abnormally shortened child spacing of about one year only. Fertile women who adopted artificial feeding for their infants, as advocated by health professionals, lost the prolonged *natural* period of infertility associated with ecological breast-feeding. Accumulated demographic data, recorded before the twentieth century from birth records all over the world, indicate that the average spacing of children was about *two* years when mother's milk supplied the major source of calories for infants during the first year to year and one-half of life.[1]

As defined and discussed in Chapter 3, ecological breast-feeding is the natural and safe, but not well-appreciated mode of child spacing. We have gradually learned to document the hormonal changes that automatically result during breast-feeding in a period or space of about two years between births.[2] The ovulation suppressant effect of ecological breast-feeding with consequent lactational amenorrhea (that is, failure to have menstrual periods while nursing) is now a well-recognized and proven fact. Two years between births is the natural "built-in" spacing time required for children to mature adequately within a family. However, the implications of this fact are only now beginning to be fully appreciated, even by experienced workers in natural family planning. The concept of lactational infertility has been difficult for most modern health professionals to accept, because their training conditions them to value technological rather than biological solutions. Their own limited experience and their experience with so many mothers of this era who only partially nursed their infants has led them to believe that controlling conceptions by breast-feeding was an old wives' tale. The scientific basis which underlies the child-spacing effect of breast-feeding has become known only recently, and has been found to be dependent on the duration, degree and frequency of the suckling stimulus.

In the past few years, through the use of highly sensitive laboratory instruments and radioactive substances, both the rate of secretion and the blood levels of hormones produced by the various endocrine glands of the body have been measured. By such means, it has been found that the pituitary hormone prolactin suppresses ovulation.[3] After birth, plasma prolactin levels differ greatly depending on whether or not the mother nurses. The secretion of prolactin has been shown to vary quantitatively with the suckling stimulus to the breast.[4] In practical terms, the level and rate of prolactin secretion varies with the number and length of feedings and the vigor of the baby. The use of pacifiers or anything that might diminish the infant's suckling automatically diminishes prolactin secretion.[5]

As far back as 1950, firm scientific evidence, from serial body temperature recordings of mothers after birth, and from repeated examination of biopsies taken from the lining of wombs (during periods of lactational amenorrhea), has shown that breast-feeding suppresses ovulation.[6] Lactation successfully suppresses ovulation when the baby sucks frequently and at short intervals (both day and night) without supplementary formula feedings or the introduction of any other foods until the baby is about six months of age. However, this natural infertility is greatly reduced if breast-feeding is partial or token, or if it is supplemented early with formula feedings or even with a too early introduction (or excessive amounts) of baby foods.[7]

An excellent review and discussion of maternal nutrition and lactational infertility was published in the medical literature in 1984.[8] These data confirm that the period of lactational amenorrhea is dependent on the duration and frequency of the suckling stimulus. In a well-controlled study in Edinburgh, a suckling frequency of "more than five times" and a duration of "more than 65 minutes" minimum (10 minutes per feed) each day was found sufficient in that population and culture to maintain complete suppression of ovarian activity.[9]

The mother's pituitary gland promptly secretes prolactin in response to nipple stimulation from the suckling child, increasing the level of prolactin in plasma 2-to 20-fold during 5 to 15 minutes of mechanical stimulation of the nipple (lactating or not), with high plasma levels being reached within 10 to 30 minutes.[10] Nursing women were shown to have much higher prolactin levels,[11] as well as lower levels of other hormones after birth, than non-nursing women.[12] Prolactin levels declined much more slowly in women who nursed more than six times a day than they did in those who nursed less frequently. Those who nursed often had no major decline in prolactin levels until about 12 months after the birth of their baby. The amount of prolactin released with suckling in the afternoon and night hours was shown to be considerably greater than in the morning hours.[13]

Interestingly, a diurnal variation in prolactin secretion during the day and night was also found to be present in non-lactating women.[14] The duration of amenorrhea and ovulation, then, is closely related both to maintaining the night feedings and to maintaining an adequate production of milk to meet the major nutritional needs of the infant.[15] These studies confirmed conclusively that ecological breast-feeding, even in industrialized countries with well-nourished mothers, will suppress fertility for a considerable period of time, ranging from about nine months to eighteen months, depending on how often the infant continues to suckle and how much milk the mother continues to produce as a result.[16]

Decrease in suckling was found to occur with the early introduction of supplementary feedings, especially when these were given in the late evening in order to prolong the period between night-time feedings. Weaning, which brings a rapid reduction in suckling (especially if it occurs after prolonged lactation), often resulted in prompt ovulation and conception when the mother was still partially nursing her baby.[17] In the August 1988 issue of *Clinical Pediatrics*, the author of this book published a review article

PROLACTIN RESPONSES TO SUCKLING AT DAY-TIME AND NIGHT-TIME FEEDS (Glasier et al, 1984)

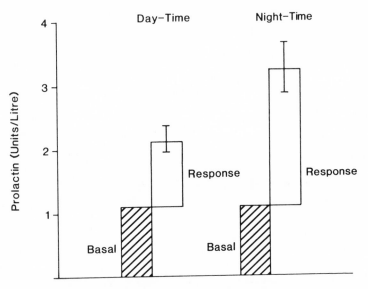

FIGURE 1: PROLACTIN RESPONSE TO NIPPLE STIMULATION.

entitled "Ecological Breast-feeding and Natural Child Spacing."[18] In this scientific review, five graphic figures were used to illustrate the fact that prolactin secretion is a reliable marker of the endocrine alterations which occur in nursing mothers after the birth of their infants. The effectiveness of nursing in continuing to suppress ovulation was seen to occur when the infants sucked frequently day and night and when only small amounts of foods were introduced gradually after the infants were about six months of age.

These five figures with their legends are reproduced here to provide a visual concept of the endocrine changes which occur and how they differ in mothers who only partially nurse as com-

PROLACTIN RESPONSES TO SUCKLING AND "HUMALACTOR"

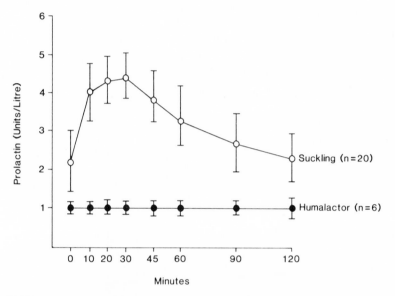

FIGURE 2: PROLACTIN LEVELS IN RESPONSE TO SUCKLING AND TO ARTIFICIAL BREAST PUMP.

pared to those who completely nurse their babies. The figures also demonstrate that the level of prolactin (PRL) is a reliable index to gauge how soon ovulation and fertily return after childbirth.

It is clear that the effect of nursing on amenorrhea and anovulation after birth varies with differing customs regarding suckling practices and the use of foods other than mother's milk, and depends, to a major extent, upon maternal understanding and motivation. In general, non-breast-feeding mothers have postpartum amenorrhea for only a few weeks, whereas truly lactating women have amenorrhea for about nine to eighteen months, depending on how often the infant suckles. The importance of natural child spacing is well summarized in the following statement by Dr. Herbert Ratner:

PROLACTIN RESPONSE TO SUCKLING (Day 5)

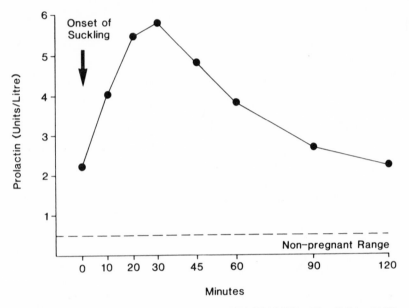

FIGURE 3: VARIATION PROLACTIN RESPONSE TO DAY AND NIGHT TIME FEEDINGS

Biological family planning (natural child spacing) from lactation amenorrhea is as old as mankind. It is nature's way of insuring an optimal period of about two years between births for children to mature within a family.[19]

Natural child spacing by breast-feeding alone, as advocated by Dr. Ratner, offers a challenging invitation to mature young couples in the following ways: (1) it brings youth to childbearing and to the arduous early child-rearing years; (2) it permits children to grow

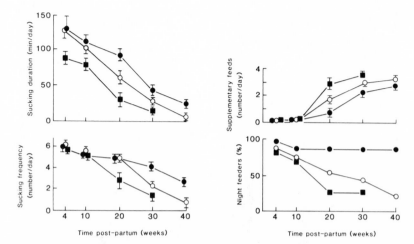

FIGURE 4: COMPARISON of SUCKLING DURATION (MEAN ± SE), SUCKLING FREQUENCY (MEAN ± SE), SUPPLEMENTARY FEEDS AND NUMBER OF NIGHT FEEDERS IN MOTHERS WHO OVULATED IN THE LATE (GREATER THAN 40 WEEKS, ●), Middle (30–40 WEEKS, O) OR EARLY (LESS THAN 30 WEEKS, ■) AFTER BIRTH.

up with a greater experience of shared intimacy; (3) it shortens the period of having preschool children who require more intensive care by the parents; (4) it closes the generation gap between parent and child, particularly valuable in the adolescent years; (5) it extends and enhances the joys of parenthood and grandparenthood; (6) it allows for a period of recovery in cases of obstetrical misfortune or tragic events; (7) it provides the couple the opportunity to re-examine their goals while reproductive options are still available; and (8) it allows them to use the *natural* prolonged period of infertility (that is, the nine months of pregnancy plus the extension by an additional year or so during ecological breast-feeding) to space their pregnancies about two years apart during their years of greatest presumed sexual activity.

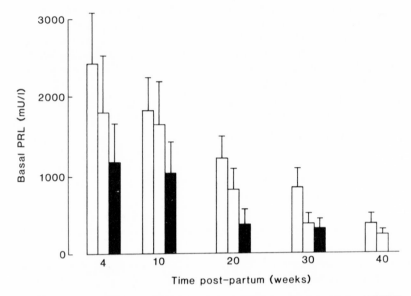

FIGURE 5: COMPARISON OF BASAL (PROLACTIN) PRL LEVELS (MEAN ± SE) IN MOTHERS WHO OVULATED IN THE LATE (OVER 40 WEEKS, ■), MIDDLE (30–40 WEEKS, □) OR EARLY (LESS THAN 3 WEEKS ■,) AFTER BIRTH.

Notes

1. J. Knodel and E. Van de Walle, "Breast-feeding, Fertility, and Infant Mortality: An Analysis of Some Early German Data," *Popula Stud.* 21:109, 1967. J. K. Van Ginneken, "Prolonged Breast-feeding as a Birth Spacing Method," *Stud. Fam. Plann.* 5:177, 1974.

2. J. Bonnar, "Effect of Breast-feeding on Pituitary-Ovarian Function After Childbirth," *Brit. Med. J.* 482–4, 1975. P. W. Howie, "Effect of Supplementary Food on Suckling Patterns and Ovarian Activity During

Lactation," *Brit. Med. Journal* 283:757, September, 1981. H. S. McNeilly, "Fertility After Childbirth: Adequacy of Post-partum Luteal Phases," *Clinical Endocrinology* 17, 609–615, 1982. R. V. Short, "Lactation: The Central Control of Reproduction," in *Breast-feeding and the Mother*, CIBA Foundation Symposium 45, pp. 73–80, Elsevier, Amsterdam, 1976. See also footnote 3.

3. R. Buchanan, "Breast-feeding: Aid to Infant Health and Fertility Control," *Popula. Rep. Ser. J.* No. 4, 1975.

4. R. W. Turkington, "Pathophysiology of Prolactin Secretion in Man," in B. L. Larson and V. H. Smith, *op. cit.* 45, vol. 2, ch. 7, p. 237. G. E. Huntington and J. A. Hostetler, "A Note on Nursing Practices in an American Isolate with a High Birth Rate," *Popula. Stud.* 24:321, 1970. See also Short, *op.cit.*, and Buchanan, *op. cit.*

5. T. J. Cronin, "Influence of Lactation upon Ovulation," *Lancet* 2:422–4, 1968. I. C. Udesky, "Ovulation in Lactating Women," *Amer. J. Obstet. Gynec.* 59:843–51, 1950.

6. J. Dobbing, *Maternal Nutrition and Lactational Infertility*. Vol. 9, Nestle Nutrition. New York: Raven Press, 1985.

7. See Short, *op. cit.*, and Bonner et al, *op. cit.*.

8. P. G. Crosignani and C. Robyn, *Prolactin and Human Reproduction*. Acad. Press, London, 1977.

9. See notes 4 and 6, above.

10. R. C. Kolodny, L. S. Jacobs and W. H. Daugheday, "Mammary Stimulation Prolactin Secretion in Non-Lactating Women," *Nature* (Lone) 238, 284–285, 1972.

11. P. Hwang, H. Guyda, H. Freisen, "Radioimmunoassay for Human Prolactin," *Proc. Natl. Acad. Sciences* 68: 1902, 1971. G. L. Noel, H. K. Suh, A. G. Frantz, "Prolactin Release During Nursing and Breast Stimulation," *J. Clin. Endocrinol Metab.* 38:413, 1974. J. E. Tyson, H. Friesen and M. S. Anderson, "Human Prolactin Studies," *Science* 177:897, 1972.

12. F. Mena, et al. "Effect of Suckling on Plasma Prolactin," *Endocrinology* 99:445, 1976. J. S. Tindal, "Hypothalamic Control of Secretion and Release of Prolactin," *J. Reprod. Fertil.* 39, 437, 1974. See also Tyson, *op. cit.*

13. D. F. Archer, and J. B. Jasinovich, "Ovarian Response to Exogenous Gonadotropins in Women with Elevated Prolactin Levels," *Obstet.*

Gynecol. 48:155, 1976. S. Jeppson, et al. "Influence of LH/FSH Releasing Hormone on the Secretion of Gonadotropins in Relation of Plasma Levels of Oestradiol, Progesterone, and Prolactin During the Post-partum Period in Lactating and in Non-Lactating Women," *Acta Endocrinol.* (Copenhagen) 84:713, 1977. R. Rolland, et al. "Hormonal Changes in Lactating Women," *Clin. Endocrin.* 4:15, 1975. See also Mena et al., *op. cit.*

14. J. F. Sassin, "Human Prolactin: 24-Hour Pattern with Increased Release During Sleep," *Science* 177:1205–7, 1973. See also footnote 5, above: Howie et al, *op. cit.*

15. See references in fooootnotes 5 and 9, above.

16. See Howie et al., *op. cit.*

17. See footnotes 4 and 6, above.

18. R. L. Jackson, "Ecological Breast-feeding and Child Spacing," *Clin. Pediatrics* 27: 373–377, 1988.

19. H. Ratner, "Child Spacing: Nature's Prescription," *Child and Family* 9:99–101, 1970.

Chapter 6

Natural Conception Regulation

To utilize lactational amenorrhea as an effective means of child spacing, it is obviously important to be able to determine reliably the return of fertility after childbirth. Though the occurrence of bleeding before the return of ovulation would be an ideal warning, this has not proved to be a reliable indicator of the return of fertility. Fertility can return before the return of menstruation. This often occurs in mothers who after a few months introduce a food supplement with the late evening nursing in order to prolong the time interval between the late evening nursing and the early morning nursing. In contrast, women who reduce the frequency of breast-feeds slowly, after the baby is about six months of age, by gradually introducing only small servings of selected foods over a period of months, are likely to have one or two infertile menstrual cycles.[1] Nature has provided an ideal way to precast the return of fertility and to delay or avoid conceptions if the couple so desire, without the use of invasive devices or chemicals.

Natural conception regulation, generally referred to as natural family planning, is the achieving or avoidance of pregnancy by the timing of intercourse based on recognition of the cyclic fertility and infertility of women. The evolution of the scientific understanding of natural conception regulation began in the early part of the nineteenth century. The mammalian ovum was first described in 1827; intermenstrual pain (abdominal pain occurring between menses) and cervical mucorrhea (a vaginal discharge of cervical mucus) were first described in 1847; and the biphasic temperature curve, that is, a thermal shift after ovulation, in 1877.[2] However, it was not until the 1950s that physicians began to combine the calculation of the number of days after menstruation with this post-ovulatory thermal shift. In the early 1950s, Dr. Joseph Roetzer, in Austria, began utilizing the onset of mucorrhea as a marker for the beginning of the fertile period, and the third day of elevated temperature readings after cessation of the mucorrhea to mark the onset of infertility after ovulation. Roetzer's studies were not published until 1968.[3] During the same time period, Dr. Edward Keefe was also utilizing mucorrhea in conjunction with temperature changes as well as self-observation of the cervix to distinguish days of possible fertility.[4]

Work on the ovulation method of natural family planning also began in the early 1950s. The first publication on this method, by Dr. John Billings of Melbourne, Australia, appeared in 1964; his book *The Ovulation Method* is now in its seventh edition.[5] Initially, Dr. Billings gave instruction in the calendar rhythm and the temperature method. Then, with the help of his wife, pediatrician Dr. Lyn Billings, he discovered that women could accurately observe, describe and record the cervical mucus pattern which indicates approaching ovulation. They could also identify the precise location of what the Billings called the "peak symptom." Consequently, the ovulation method evolved, in which progressive changes in the cervical mucus are identified by the feeling produced by the mucus at the vulva and by its visual appearance, to provide a simple, natural method of recognizing the phases of fertility and infertility.[6] A World Health Organization Committee suggested calling this ovulation method after the pioneering research team. The Billings Method is now taught and used effectively in over one hundred countries.

In 1968, Mercedes Arzu Wilson learned the ovulation method from the Drs. Billings. At that time the observations of the cervical mucus were taught together with temperature readings, in what is known today as the sympto-thermal method. However, when Mrs. Wilson brought the ovulation method to her native country of Guatemala in 1970 and began teaching amongst the poor, she realized that she could not teach the temperature method to her people, as the majority were illiterate. Consequently, she devised a multicolored charting system, using red stamps to indicate days of menstrual bleeding, brown stamps for days of dryness, when there is no cervical secretion, and white stamps with an imprint of a baby during the days of fertility when the white cervical secretion is present in the woman's body. This simple charting system proved so effective that when Mrs. Wilson invited the Drs. Billings to teach in Guatemala and Central America in 1970 and showed them its practicality and efficacy, the Billings decided to adopt it in Australia and beyond, as its use expanded around the world.

During the 1950s and 1960s, Dr. Ronald Prem, Professor of Obstetrics and Gynecology at the University of Minnesota, undertook a critical analysis of the basal temperature graphs of women under his observation to discover why certain mothers using natural family planning had become pregnant.[7] His objective was to increase effectiveness in teaching couples natural family planning. In 1971, the Kippleys, under the guidance of Professor Prem, established the Couple to Couple League. The purpose of the CCL was to develop a network of professionally-trained teaching couples to teach natural family planning (the sympto-thermal method and ecological breast-feeding) in both urban neighborhoods and rural counties in the United States. The Kippleys also saw the need for an instruction manual; *The Art of Natural Family Planning* is now in its fourth edition.

The discovery and availability of isotopes (radioactive substances) made it possible to measure accurately the hormonal changes occurring during the natural phases of fertility and infertility in women's menstrual cycles. Long-term clinical studies were then undertaken to correlate these hormonal changes with objectively detectable physical signs. Gradually it has become possible to understand more fully the physiology of the menstrual cycle.

Natural conception regulation, an integral part of natural family planning, is based on the biological fact that a woman is fertile for only a few days before and after ovulation. A healthy male is presumed to be constantly fertile. Understanding and carefully observing the woman's natural signs of fertility enables a couple to more accurately achieve pregnancy by having sexual intercourse when these signs are present or to avoid pregnancy by abstaining from sexual contact during that time. Natural conception regulation by the methods now available can be used throughout a woman's entire reproductive lifetime: during both regular and irregular menstrual cycles, after childbirth, during breast-feeding and premenopause, or after discontinuation of birth control pills. During ecological breast-feeding, natural conception regulation occurs via natural fertility regulation, as previously explained.

Both the sympto-thermal and ovulation methods of natural fertility regulation as opposed to the old "calendar rhythm system" have a method effectiveness of 98 to 99%. while use effectiveness ranges from 76 to 98%, depending greatly on the motivation of the couple to avoid pregnancy.[10]

Unlike artificial methods, natural conception regulation (NCR) offers the added advantage of aiding couples who want to conceive a child to know the time of maximum fertility as well as almost the exact date of conception. To learn NCR, motivation to adhere to the method is needed as well as a brief but intensive period of instruction. The couple has to learn by fully grasping a few basic facts and gaining first-hand practical experience. Couple need to master the method most suited to their lifestyle, and not just know *about* different methods. Accurate observation and recording skills can be greatly enhanced under the guidance of a competent teacher. However, we now have excellent teaching manuals so simple and well-illustrated that motivated intelligent couples can master NCR by themselves. One of the best manuals is *Love and Fertility*, developed by Mercedes Wilson, executive director of the Family of the Americas Foundation, Inc.

Throughout the course of each menstrual cycle a woman has easily detectable and quite reliable signs that indicate her times of fertility. Observed on a day-to-day basis, these symptoms and signs provide current information about what is happening here and now during the present cycle. Fertility awareness means learning to define the times of fertility and infertility in relationship to the occurrence of symptoms and signs in the course of the menstrual cycle. The onset of the fertile phase is signalled by the appearance of cervical mucus, which is initiated when the hormone (estrogen) secreted by the ovary reaches a certain level. The cervical mucus greatly facilitates sperm transport and is capable of maintaining sperm survival from 48 to 72 hours, and possibly longer. Cervical mucus can not only be observed as a normal vaginal discharge during the woman's daily personal hygiene but anytime she directs attention to the sensations of her body. By learning to discern the differences in her own pattern of mucus discharge, a woman can reliably know when she is presumably fertile and when she is not.

Once the egg has been released from the ovary (in the process called ovulation), progesterone is secreted, rapidly shutting off the cervical mucus and causing a significant rise in basal body temperature. A woman's waking body temperature rises to a higher level very close to the time of ovulation and stays high for about two weeks, until her next menstrual period. By observing this pattern of temperature rise, postovulatory infertility can be determined with relative certainty, although there are slight differences of opinion as to how to identify precisely when this infertility period begins. A number of formulas are advocated by different experienced physicians for computing the onset of postovulatory infertility. Roetzer[12] considers the peak mucus sign as critical and does not begin the count of three elevated temperature days' readings until the peak day is passed. Consequently, if a couple has a serious medical reason to avoid conception (e.g., if the wife has vascular complications from diabetes), it would be advisable and prudent for such a couple to use the most conservative formula and confine intercourse to the postovulatory period of infertility.

Two major methods of teaching and practicing natural conception regulation have evolved. The first is known as the ovulation method (OM) and the second as the sympto-thermal method (STM). The OM proponents such as Billings, Klaus and Hilgers [13] have compiled extensive data to indicate that most couples can achieve effective and acceptable conception regulation on the basis of external mucus observations alone, provided each couple is instructed to observe, interpret and recored the buildup pattern of the normal fertile mucus, in keeping with their individual needs. OM proponents sometimes use basal body temperature readings as a temporary learning tool under the guidance of a competent teacher to help clear up ambiguity, so that eventually the couple can be confident using only progressive changes in the mucus. In general, the simplicity of the OM method has led to its being preferred by teachers and users, especially in the developing world.

Proponents of the sympto-thermal method believe that to make conception regulation more acceptable and universal, most couples should be informed about all the signs and symptoms, including basal body temperature readings, and under the guidance of an instructor, be allowed to discover from their own experience which signs they ultimately prefer to use. They contend that "combining signs" provides greater understanding, especially for the husband, and allows different signs and symptoms to compensate for the weakness of others. The sympto-thermal method is preferred by some NFP teachers, and especially by users living in the more developed areas of the world, where couples with more formal education have been taught how to observe the signs and chart their observations. Learning the sympto-thermal method can provide educated couples with additional objective signs for both husband and wife to observe when ovulation has occurred, and confirms that the period of infertility after ovulation remains relatively constant and predictable in each menstrual cycle.

Those who prefer the ovulation method as the primary technique for instruction consider that teaching "multiple indicators" of varying degrees of reliability makes the learning process more difficult and the daily recording more time-consuming. Confusion and discouragement may occur when the less reliable indicators appear to "contradict" the information provided by the mucus pattern. If there is initial difficulty, perhaps because of anxiety over some pathological disorder, an additional indicator may be provided as a temporary help. Particularly recommended is the use by teaching centers of the comparatively simple technology of the ovarian monitor devised by Professor James B. Brown of Melbourne, Australia, for measuring the ovarian hormonal pattern.[14]

When a natural method is used to achieve pregnancy, the number of cycles necessary to achieve the desired pregnancy is recorded. While the majority of users who understand their fertility patterns can achieve pregnancy in one or two cycles, a range of up to ten cycles is still considered to be within normal limits.[15]

Obviously the "procreative choice" (family planning intention) must be recorded at each follow-up in order to evaluate the effectiveness of the methods. When considering the efectiveness of natural conception regulation, we should never forget that every child conceived is a mystery. What technological means do we have for measuring such a marvel as human life at the time of conception? We should not be afraid to have a sense of the sacred, and admit that as human beings seeking the truth, there always remain mites of the unknown which are shrouded in mystery.

I quote the following statement of Dr. Hanna Klaus, who has had extensive international experience with natural family planning and has directed attention to helping couples resolve the problems of periodic abstinence which natural conception regulation entails.

It is clear that natural family planning users do not isolate their procreative capacity out of their person; therefore, if they intend to use the method for avoidance of pregnancy, abstinence during the fertile phase is essential. Many users need to learn periodic abstinence. Even though learners are self-selected, they may still experience learning difficulties. Teacher-client dialogue is essential, although some programs confine themselves to inspection of the woman's chart and are then open to questions. Couples who have previously taken constant sexual availability for granted may find it very difficult to learn how to deal with abstinence. This dimension has appeared to be very formidable to those who have assumed that people find sexual abstinence very difficult, and therefore think that family planning methods which require the least motivation are most likely to be used. This has not been the experience of physicians who have taught natural family planning. Beyond the normal anxiety about learning new material and launching from (perceived) security to insecurity, women in particular may feel that their husbands may not be pleaseed to be told that intercourse is not available. Generally, within two cycles the couple has discovered thay they're not saying "no" to each other, but that they're saying "we're fertile and we have decided we do not want to try for a baby this month." This is not a rejection of the person but a recognition of the couple's fertility.

Many family planning providers assume that couple in Third World countries do not have discussions about sex. A cross-cultural NFP acceptor study (in the U.S.A., India, South Korea, Bangladesh and Kenya) found that spouses ask each other if they wish to have intercourse. After exposure to the education program, cooperation is the rule rather than the exception. The key to success is the recognition by the couple that expressions of conjugal love can be far wider than genital intercourse. It is the task of the teacher in follow-up to make tactful inquiries to find out whether the couples are comfortable with whatever conjugal dialogue occurs during the fertile phase and whether they were able to wait for the end of the fertile phase. Most couples reach autonomy within two or three months of beginning the program, but everyone occasionally finds difficulties. If the desire to avoid another pregnancy is strong, couples find other non-genital expressions of mutual love.[16]

Natural family planning involves couples in a whole new approach to family planning. The normal healthy processes of fertility are understood, accepted and lived with, instead of being disrupted with the real potential for producing pathological changes. And, because of the shared commitment to be responsible together for a fertility that is "ours" (not "hers"), mutual respect and trust can flourish.

As more doctors have become increasingly concerned with technology, some ecologists are beginning to realize that fertility is a normal physiological event and therefore it is logical and desirable to use symptoms and signs to educate couples regarding procreative choice. While the hormonal changes (endocrinology) of fertility and their relationship to the signs and symptoms of the markers of fertility have been well-established, the critical factor is the motivation as well as the understanding of the user. Rather than consider any conception as a failure, as would be appropriate if one is using a method whose only purpose was to isolate the fertility out of the body while still permitting sexual intercourse, these natural methods of conception leave fertility intact.

A conference of natural family planning physician-researchers applied the term "informed choice pregnancy" to those pregnancies which were engendered by couples who knowingly use the fertile phase. Many couple are ambivalent about when to have another child. "Informed choice" pregnancies were few (only about 2%) when couple were serious about avoiding pregnancies[17] and relatively frequent (about 25%) when they were not.[18] The term "teaching related pregnancy" was applied to those who had a basic misunderstanding of methodology. In the face of competent instruction, teaching related pregnancies should be and in fact are few and far between.[19] In the absence of sufficient information to classify, other pregnancies are termed "unresolved pregnancy."

In summary, modern natural conception regulation is based on proven scientific and medical research, using physiological "markers" to determine the beginning and end of the fertile phase of each menstrual cycle. Unlike the old calendar rhythm method, the new methods are much more precise, and can be used by all women (whatever their individual pattern). They are applicable to puberty, lactation, weaning, and premenopause. Natural methods are a "first-line" approach for infertility studies. Although the initial learning requres close attention to accurate observations, there are no continuing costs. They have no harmful side effects, and the couple retains freedom of procreative choice. They place equal responsibility for conception control *on both the husband and wife*; with proper instruction and guidance, couple autonomy can be achieved. The discipline required for proper use of a natural method actually promotes mutual love of husband and wife through the shared responsibility of their combined fertility. Natural methods are as effective as any other method of birth control when correctly understood and properly used. They are also a way of responsibile parenthood acceptable to all religions and cultures.[20]

Notes

1. J. Bonnar, et al. "Effect of Breast-feeding on Pituitary-Ovarian Functions after Childbirth," *British Medical Journal* 4:82–4, 1975.

2. R. Vollman, *Natural Family Planning: Introduction to Methods* (ed. C. Ross) Washington, D. C.: Human Life Foundation, 1977.

3. J. Roetzer, "Erweiterte Basalt Temperatur-Messung und Empfangnis Regelung," *Arch. Gynaekol.* 206:195, 1968.

4. E. F. Keefe, "Self-observation of the Cervix to Distinguish Days of Possible Fertility," *Bulletin of the Sloane Hospital for Women* VII:129–136 (Dec. 1962).

5. J. J. Billings, *The Ovulation Method* Melbourne: Advocate Press, 1964 (7th edition, 1983).

6. E. L. and J. J. Billings, "Symptoms and Hormonal Changes Accompanying Ovulation," *Lancet* 1:282, 1982.

7. K. Prem, "Basal Temperature Method," *Proc. of 2nd International Symposium on Rhythm.* Washington, D. C. Family Life Bureau, 1968 (pp.47–64). Reprinted in *Child and Family* 7:311–327, 1968.

8. J. F. and S. K. Kippley, *The Art of Natural Famiily Planning.* Cincinnati: Couple to Couple League, 1984. Couple to Couple League, P. O. Box 11184, Cincinnati, Ohio, 45211.

9. H. Klaus, "Natural Family Planning: A Review," *Obstetrical and Gynecological Survey* 37: 127–159. Baltimore: The Williams and Wilkins, Co., 1982. See also footnotes 3 and 6, above.

10. T. W. Hilgers, A. M. Prebil and K. D. Daly, *The Effectiveness of the Ovulation Method.* Creighton University, NFP Research Center, Omaha, 1980. J. F. Kippley, "The Effectiveness of Natural Family Planning," *The Couple to Couple League News* XII: 5, 1986. J. Roetzer, "The Sympto-Thermal Method: Ten Years of Change," *Linacre Quarterly* 45:358, 1978. See also footnotes 3 and 6, above.

11. Family of the Americas Foundation, Inc. 1150 Lovers Lane, P. O. Box 219, Mandeville, Louisiana, 70448. This excellent teaching manual is available in many languages.

12. J. Roetzer, *Fine Points of the Sympto-Thermal Method of NFP* (Suppl. E.F. Keefe), Arnold Family Planning Center, Nagoya, Japan, 1977.

13. T. W. Hilgers, *The Ovulation Method of Natural Family Planning, PS.* Creighton University; second edition, 1983. See Billings, *op. cit.*, and Klaus, *op. cit.*

14. J. B. Brown, P. Harrison and M. A. Smith "A Study of Returning Fertility after Childbirth and during Lactation by Measurement of Uri-

nary Estrogen and Pregnanediol Excretion and Cervical Mucus Production," *Journal of the Biosoc. Sci.* Suppl. 9: 5-23, 1985.

15. H. Klaus and M. Fagan, "Natural Family Planning," *JAMA* 37: 231-241, 1982.

16. H. Klaus, Personal communication, 1988.

17. "All India Documentation and Evaluation Report, Natural Family Planning Programme in India," New Delhi, Indian Government Social Services Society, 1981.

18. P. D. Darney, "New Developments in Barrier Contraception," *Sexual Medicine Today* 9: 3: 5-9, 1985.

19. H. Klaus and M. Fagan "Natural Family Planning: Analysis of Change in Procreative Intention," *JAMA* 37: 231-241, 1982.

20. In September 1989, the International Journal of Gynecology and Obstetrics published a supplemental issue to cover a recent symposium on the natural regulation of fertility sponsored by three Roman university medical schools, two Pontifical Universities, and the World Health Organization. The articles presented provide current scientific data and an extensive bibliography to support the vital importance of natural conception regulation as reviewed in this chapter. "Natural Fertility Regulation Today," *International Journal of Gynecology and Obstetrics* Suppl. 1: 1-167, 1989.

Chapter 7

Birth Control

Between 1850 and 1930, the world population doubled—to about two billion. There were many reasons for this rapid increase in population, but it resulted primarily from environmental changes, including more rational public health measures for better control of infectious diseases, especially in infants and children. The survival of millions of infants and children into childbearing ages meant that there were many more young parents producing children; in addition there were also many adults who were living longer.

Overpopulation first became the subject of intellectual concern with the publication in 1798 of *An Essay of the Principle of Population*, by Thomas Malthus. His basic thesis was that population tends to increase faster than food resources. In the 1860s, a Malthusian League was founded in England, and contraception information began to be disseminated in Western culture.[1]

In the latter part of the nineteenth century, improved forms of condoms and diaphragms became available.

By the twentieth century, the birth control movement had become international. In 1927, the first World Conference on Population was held in Geneva, and in 1930, the first international clinic advocating contraceptive methods was opened in Zurich. Margaret Sanger pioneered the movement in the United States in 1913,[2] and by 1931, so-called birth control clinics in the United States were dispensing instructions on unnatural ways to control conception. By 1935, over 200 types of mechanical devices were being used; in addition, a wide variety of chemical solutions were available as spermicides. There were also progressive advances in technology and in the commercial availability of contraceptives.

Artificial methods of birth control include:

(1) Barrier techniques which block sperm from entering the uterus (condoms, diaphragms, cervical caps, etc.).

(2) Spermatocides, which kill sperm in the vagina.

(3) Synthetic chemicals (birth control pills or injectables), which simulate the action of natural hormones on the reproductive sustem so as to a) suppress ovulation (medical sterilization) by creating hostile endometrium, which prevents implantation of the fertilized egg (abortifacient), and b) thicken the cervical mucus to prevent passage of the sperm into the uterus (contraceptive). The high-dosage "combined" birth control pill had as its major effect anovulation (medical sterilization). As the dosage decreases, the abortifacient effect increases—rendering the birth control pill primarily an abortifacient. The minipill (progestin only) is also primarily abortifacient, and is "associated with a higher frequency of certain side effects and unwanted pregnancy than the combination . . . pill."[3]

(4) IUDs (intrauterine devices), which disrupt implantation to cause abortions which are earlier and miniature in nature.

(5) Medical abortifacient pills which kill the young embryo by disrupting its support system, e.g., RU 486. (These newer forms of birth control pills are resulting in national and international conflicts.)

(6) Surgical abortion.

(7) Surgical sterilization: tubal ligation in the female, and vasectomy in the male.

At the same time as these artificial methods of contraception were being developed and promoted, a natural method of controlling conceptions was also introduced. The natural method of regulating conceptions (calendar rhythm method) was based on the studies of reproductive physiology of Dr. Kyusaku Ogino (1924,Ja-

pan)[4] and Dr. Herman Knaus, (1929, Austria).[5] Working independently, they found that most women ovulated about two weeks
before the beginning of their next menstrual period. The formulas
advocated for conception regulation based only on calendar
rhythm provided no reliable method to determine the relatively
frequent minor and major normal variations that occur in the fertility cycles from month to month in many women. Nevertheless,
the basic findings discovered by and introduced by Drs. Ogino
and Knaus were sound. The effectiveness of this natural method
of conception regulation for married couples who tried to abide by
their directions was between 60 and 80 percent. However, because
the rhythm method was relatively unreliable and required periodic
abstinence from sexual intercourse, it was not advocated by many
doctors and was unacceptable to most couples.

From 1920 to 1935, artificial barrier methods of conception control were gradually approved by many physicians. In the 1920s,
articles pertaining to various methods of conception control began
to appear in the American and European medical journals, articles
that provoked considerable debate as to the desirability and safety
of these methods.[6] By 1933, when the author was a medical stu-
dent, most if not all, medical schools began defining indications
for and advising various contraceptive techniques. The change in
medical opinion paralleled similar changes of opinion in other
fields, especially sociology and economics, and in the mass media.
However, many professionals in various disciplines opposed such
changes. Opponents were successful in updating the old 1873
Comstock law[7] which forbade the sending through the mails of
". . . any drug or medicine or article whatever for the prevention of
conception; the advertisement of such articles through the mails;
their importation into the United States; or their manufacture,
sale, or possession in the District of Columbia and federal territo-
ries . . ." Up to ten years' imprisonment was stipulated for viola-
tion of the section on mailing, with lesser penalties for other acts.
Opposition to artificial birth control methods remained sufficiently
strong in 1930 to secure the re-enactment of the provision against
importation of contraceptives in the Tariff Act of that year. However, in the same year, the Court of Appeals held that a manufac-

turer of condoms was not engaged in an illegal activity. In 1936, the same court permitted the importation of contraceptives by a doctor, maintaining that Congress had meant only to prohibit the "immoral use" of contraceptives, and that use prescribed by a physician was not immoral. A final step was taken by the Post Office Department in 1958 when it announced that it would not ban the mailing of contraceptives if they were not destined for "unlawful purposes." In each situation, the impracticability of distinguishing between medical uses and "immoral" or "illegal uses" made enforcement of the law impossible.

Through the years, not only medical and legal, but also religious opinions changed. In 1908 and in 1920, the Lambeth Conference of Anglican Bishops in England condemned artificial contraception. In America, in 1925, the House of Bishops of the Protestant Episcopal Church also condemned it. However, in 1930, the Lambeth Conference, despite the determined opposition of a minority, adopted the following resolution:

> Where there is a clearly-felt moral obligation to limit or avoid parenthood, the method must be decided on Christian principles. The primary and obvious method is complete abstinence from intercourse (as far as may be necessary) in a life of discipline and self-control lived in the power of the Holy Spirit. Nevertheless in those cases where there is such a clearly-felt moral obligation to limit or avoid parenthood, and where there is a morally sound reason for avoiding complete abstinence, the conference agrees that other methods may be used, provided that this is done in the light of the same Christian principles. The Conference records its strongest condemnation of the use of any methods of conception control from motives of selfishness, luxury, or mere convenience.

After the Anglican decision in 1930, a large number of other Christian churches publicly abandoned the absolute prohibition of contraception by married couples. The various religious bodies which changed their stand were: the Congregational Christian General Council (1931); the General Council of the United Church of Canada (1936); the Methodist Conference of Great Britain (1939); the British Council of Churches (1943); a special commission of the Church of Scotland (1944); the bishops of the (Lutheran) Church of Sweden (1951); the General Synod of the Netherlands Reformed Church (1952); the General Conference of the Methodist Church in the United States (1956); the United Lutheran Church in the United States (1956); the International Convention of the Disciples of Christ (1958); and the World Council of Churches (1959).[8]

However, the Catholic Church maintained opposition to the unnatural birth control movement. In 1930, Pope Pius XI issued *Casti Connubii*. The encyclical was a small *summa* on Christian marriage, and distilled doctrinal statements as they had been transmitted from the beginning through Judeo-Christian tradition.

The introduction in the late 1950s and 1960s of oral hormonal medications (birth control pills) as a non-barrier method of contraception precipitated speculation that the Church might modify its teaching on birth control. Pope John XXIII appointed a commission to study the problem. The commission was unable to reach an agreement, and formulated controversial opinions which were presented to Pope Paul VI. After studying the commission's reports and obtaining additional opinions, the pope decided to reaffirm the nineteen centuries of Christian teaching against unnatural forms of conception regulation.[10] The stance of the Catholic Church since that time will be the focus of the next chapter.

The birth control pill was licensed in the United States on May 11, 1960, and was introduced as highly effective, which it was, and as a method which was "natural and physiological," which it was not. The latter belief resulted in negligible testing for safety prior to marketing. By early 1961, reports of deaths and thromboembolic complications began trickling in, first in the British and later in the American medical literature. Some isolated voices, particularly that of Dr. Herbert Ratner, at that time Public Health Director of Oak Park, Illinois, began warning women of the pill's dangers. Complications and deaths from the pill slowly but steadily kept mounting. In 1968, under the caption "Recent Setbacks in Medicine," the medical hazards of using the birth control pills were reviewed in detail in *Child and Family Quarterly* (this article was subsequently issued in book form in 1969.) The book showed that the pill was the most poorly tested drug that had ever been introduced for use by healthy women. Three other books, all critical of the pill, also appeared in 1969: *The Pill: An Alarming Report;*[12] *Pregnant or Dead?;*[13] and *The Doctor's Case Against the Pill.*[14] From the beginning, however, powerful forces kept denying, explaining away, or minimizing the dangers of the pill and the pill acquired a "diplomatic immunity" which has persisited to the present. Even so, controversy over the safety of the pill continued, and gave rise to the famous Nelson Senate Hearings in 1970, during which Dr. Ratner testified that the pill was "chemical warfare against the women of the world."[15]

Following the Nelson Hearings the drug companies began promoting pills with the smallest possible effective chemical concentrations, in an attempt to reduce complications. Experienced endocrinologists should have known, however, that the use of powerful synthetic chemicals in healthy women to alter nature is unphysiological and contraindicated. In our first pharmacologic lecture in medical school (in my case, in 1930), students were taught that you never give drugs to well people to make them sick; rather, you give medicine to sick people to make them well.

The fact is that synthetic chemicals simulating natural sex hormones also affect every part of the body. The goal of natural hormones is the maintainance of function, whereas the goal of the synthetic chemicals is to produce dysfunction. It should be understood that the so-called "side effects" of the pill are in reality the effects of the pill. There is no way of completely isolating the desired effect from the undesired effects by reducing dosage in the combined pill (which contains estrogens and progestins) or by removing one of the two synthetic chemicals, as is attempted in another type of minipill. Furthermore, reduction of the dosage in the combined pill reduces its effectiveness. It decreases the pill's primary mode of action, the suppression of ovulation (sterilization), and increases its secondary mode of action, the prevention of implantation of a fertilized egg in the uterus (early abortion). The reason for this is that nature is baffled when it comes to metabolizing or ridding the body of chemicals. Clinical evidence is accumulating that minipills also have serious long-term complications.[16]

As early as 1962, the late Doctor Carl Hartman, an authority in reproductive physiology wrote, "No physician should refuse to teach the best methods for determining the fertile period to couples who request the instruction."[17] Most physicians have ignored this sound advice. In fact, few physicians and allied health workers are at present knowledgeable about the scientific advances in natural conception regulation.

In 1985, two West German physicians, Drs. Petra Frank and Elizabeth Raith, published *Natural Family Planning: Physiological Bases, Method Comparison, and Effectiveness*, for physicians and counselors. The goal of the book, as stated in the foreword by Dr. G. Doehring, Professor and Chief of Obstetrics and Gynecology at Munich City Hospital, is to present the scientific foundation for the various modern methods of NFP and to present a critical evaluation of their reliability. This new book contains an excellent current bibliography, and should be useful for re-educating the health professions.[18]

The contributions of many research centers throughout the world are advancing our knowledge and understanding of human reproductive physiology. Examples of such centers in the United States include the recent Pope Paul VI Institute for the Study of Human Reproduction at Creighton University in Omaha, Nebraska, under the direction of Dr. Thomas Hilgers, Associate Clinical Professor of Obstetrics and Gynecology at Creighton University, and the Natural Family Planning Center of Washington, D.C., under the direction of Dr. Hanna Klaus, F.A.C.O.G., Associate Clinical Professor of OB/GYN of the George Washington University Medical Center. Many similar programs on local, regional, national, and international levels also exist and are expanding. These natural family planning programs are not only extending services, but also providing new insights as to how to teach most effectively what to whom.

Daily monitoring of the signs of fertility and infertility allows a woman to more readily identify potential pathology and to report her observations promptly to her physician. Body awareness helps her to understand changes in mood and energy levels during various phases of her menstrual cycle. As Dr. Klaus has said, "it takes an intellectual reorientation to conclude that choosing when and if to try to conceive a baby is more logical and human than merely taking an oral tablet, using a device or submitting to contraceptive sterilization."[19]

Research continues to enable us to find more precise indices for identifying the time of ovulation. However, to date, no new technological procedures, such as more definitive changes in temperature readings, measurement of vaginal fluids, or the calibration of cervical mucus volume or hormone levels in urine, have been found to be more reliable than the experienced woman's self-observation.

Highly subsidized public and private birth control clinics have and are advising some women, concerned about the safety of artificial methods, how to identify their fertile period by mucus observations and then to use barrier techniques only during their fertile period. In addition, some clinics also instruct their clients to use the thermal shift to help decide when to discontinue the use of contraceptives. However, the use of such techniques, especially if foams or diaphragms are used, can confuse the true signs of fertility by modifying the cervical mucus, thus making it a less reliable marker of the time of ovulation. Consequently, many couples using sometimes artificial, sometimes natural methods have found the practice neither satisfying nor reliable. Couples using the artificial but often designated "natural" method have done much to discredit the high degree of reliability of true natural conception regulation.

Engagement in intercourse during the fertile phase, using a condom, a diaphragm or withdrawal as a contraceptive method, is not combining such a technique with the natural method, but actually changing from one technique to the other, because to be effective, the natural method would demand the avoidance of genital contact at this time, if it were the couple's intention to avoid pregnancy. This is the only time in the cycle when it is possible for the woman to become pregnant, and it is obvious that the avoidance of genital contact is the only reliable way to avoid pregnancy, in preference to a contraceptive method which has a substantial failure rate.

Notes

1. Himes. *Medical History of Contraception*. New York: Alan F. Guttmacher, Gamet Press, 1963, p. 238.

2. M. Sanger, *An Autobiography*. New York: Daves Publications, Inc., 1971.

3. T. W. Hilgers, "The Intrauterine Device: Contraceptive or Abortifacient?" *Minnesota Med.* 491-501, June 1974.

4. K. Ogino, *Conception Period of Women* (English Translation). Harrisburg, PA, 1934.

5. H. Knaus, "Period Fertility and Sterility," in *Women's Vienna*, 1933.

6. J. T. Noonan, *Contraception*. Cambridge: Harvard University Press, 1965.

7. "The History and Future of the Legal Battle over Birth Control," *Cornell Law Quarterly* 257-277, 1963.

8. See Noonan, *op. cit.*

9. Pius XI, *Casti Connubii*, Vatican, December, 1930.

10. Paul VI, *Humanae Vitae* (new translation), San Francisco: Ignatius Press, 1978.

11. H. Ratner, *The Medical Hazards of the Birth Control Pills*. Child and Family Reprint Booklet Series, 1969.

12. M. N. Mintz, *The Pill: An Alarming Report*. Boston: Beacon Press, 1970.

14. H. Williams, *Pregnant or Dead? The Pill in New Perspective*. San Francisco: New Perspective Publications, 1969 (reprinted in *Child and Family*, vol. 1-vol. 15 No. 3, 1975-1976.)

14. B. Seeman, *The Doctor's Case Against the Pill*. New York: Van Rees Press, 1969.

15. C. H. Ratner, "The Nelson Hearings on Oral Contraceptives—Testimony," reprinted in *Child and Family* 9: 349-376, 1970.

16. V. Beral, "Mortality Among Oral Contraceptive Users," *Lancet* 727-731, October, 1977. Food and Drug Administration. "Oral Contraceptive Drug Products," *Federal Register* 41:236, December 1976 (536341). C. Hartman, *Science and the Safe Period*. Baltimore: Williams and

Wilkins, 1962. Hume, K. *Human Love and Human Life*. Polding Press, 1979. S. Shapiro, "Oral Contraceptives—Time to Take Stock," *New Engl. J. Med.* 1986.

17. See Hartman, *op. cit.*

18. Huneger Book Review, *International Review Natural Family Planning* Vol. 12, No. 4, pp. 349, 1985.

19. H. Klaus, Personal communication, 1988.

Chapter 8

The Catholic Church and Birth Control

It is notable that in his letter On Human Life, the late Pope Paul VI predicted that a culture that accepts artificial contraception would eventually accept abortion. He also indicated that contraception degraded women. Now, more than twenty years later, many women seem to be beginning to appreciate his insight. Though many Catholic theologians disagreed with Paul VI's 1968 encyclical *Humanae Vitae*, the cumulative evidence of the negative consequences of unnatural methods of birth control, especially intrauterine devices and birth control pills, supports his decision to reject such artificial interventions.

The present Pope, John Paul II, has written extensively to defend and clarify the teachings of the Church on human life. In fact, during his general weekly audiences between July to November, 1984, Pope John Paul II reviewed in depth and interpreted all of the issues treated by Pope Paul VI in *Humanae Vitae*[1]

In those weekly audiences, John Paul II explained why the self-possession of the person should be understood in terms of "self-donation," not merely in terms of the person's rights, but of their responsibilities. On this basis, he convincingly outlined the essential merits of the unitive and the procreative aspects of sexual union. His reflections upon and interpretation of *Humanae Vitae* make it easier to understand that the sexual union of spouses, when deprived of its procreative possibility, is no longer an expression of spousal self-donation. In fact, it becomes directly opposed to self-donation. The possibility of procreation must remain open, if the spouses are to give themselves to each other without reserve and without compromising their love. To put it another way, contraception is a negation of both the wholeness of the self and the wholeness of the sex act. This concept substantiates the equal rights of both sexes.

Although women and men are equal in dignity, they differ substantially from one another in order to complement each other. They differ not only anatomically and physiologically but also psychologically. The differences of function are not arbitrary but are the result of a different balance and sequence of sex hormones which reflect their very beings. The vocation of women is very far from being limited to bringing healthy infants into the world and breast-feeding them. However, a mother is connatural to her children in a very special psychological and physical way which permits repeated daily acts of understanding and love which are indispensable to raising a child effectively, especiallly during infancy and the preschool years.

Father Richard Huneger, Archdiocesan Director of Pastoral Services in Portland, Oregon, outlines the progression of John Paul II's interpretation of *Humanae Vitae* in this fashion:

(1) Human beings are masculine or feminine *persons*.
(2) These persons are in the *image* of God.
(3) Together they have the power of *transmitting* the image of God (conceiving, giving birth, and nurturing natural and supernatural life).
(4) The only *place* worthy of sexual intercourse is the relationship of proclaimed, lifelong committed love (in marriage).
(5) Marriage is understood in terms of *total mutual self-donation*, which is *freely* bestowed.
(6) To act freely presupposes the ability to say *yes or no*.
(7) Therefore freedom is proportionate to *self-possession*.
(8) Freedom in sexual self-giving is proportionate to self-possession in the relations between the masculine and feminine persons; the *virtue* proper to this dimension of self-possession is *continence*.

(9) Continence, as it matures, transforms the relationship from one of *excitement* (pre-reflective "craving" or "desire") to one of *emotion* (reflective "regard" or "cherishing"). The excitement from "taking" and "getting" a "part" of the other person is transformed and integrated into a mutual "bestowing" and "receiving" of the "whole" of each person in the totality of masculinity and femininity. The act is truly free, mutual self-donation.

(10) Self-determination, through self-possession, assisted by continence, means that excitement is channeled by emotion in ways that respect the full nuptial meaning of the body; thus, fornication and adultery are excluded, as well as contraception, while the range of ways in which *affection* is expressed encompasses nongenital as well as genital ways (the former being needed by all persons, married or not; the latter being proper to marriage but not the exclusive way of expressing affection in marriage).

Pope John Paul II also stressed that it is morally lawful to have recourse to the woman's infertile periods, if there are sound reasons for spacing births or even grave reasons for preventing births, and in this way to control births without offending moral principles. He made it clear that there is an essential difference of an ethical nature between natural and unnatural methods. In natural conception regulation, the married couple by self-discipline use a facility provided them by nature, while with artificial methods, they selfishly obstruct the natural functioning of the generative process.

It is the author's conviction that a major factor in the consideration and selection of Cardinal Karol Woytyla as Pope was the recognition of his understanding and teachings of human sexuality and their fostering of the preservation of family life. No doubt it was his pastoral concern for his university students that stimulated him to study human sexuality in depth so as to more fully understand the basis for the consistent traditional Judeo-Christian teachings as stated by Paul VI in *Humanae Vitae*.

A few years prior to Vatican II, the author's bishop invited him along with two other physicians to discuss with him and his clergy their concerns about the dangers of accepting artificial methods of contraception. This meeting took place during the period when the commission appointed by the Holy See was considering the problem of birth control. The two other doctors were Dr. Herbert Ratner, then Professor of Preventive Medicine at Loyola University Medical School, in Chicago, Illinois, editor of *Child and Family* and President of the National Federation of Catholic Physician's Guild, and Dr. John Hillabrand of Toledo, Ohio, an obstetrician and nationally recognized authority on natural family planning. Over the course of three days, we three doctors held lively and challenging discussions with small groups of priests from Bishop Joseph Marling's Jefferson City, Missouri diocese. We readily substantiated our belief that the Judeo-Christian traditional teachings on human sexuality were in jeopardy.

Later, after actively participating in Vatican II, Bishop Marling told me, "Dr. Bob, I want to tell you that while I was in Rome, I met and became acquainted with a very impressive young bishop named Karol Woytyla. He really does understand what you three doctors reviewed with me and my priests so that we could better understand and somewhat more effectively defend the traditional teachings of the church relating to human sexuality."

In *Familaris Consortio* (*The Role of the Christian Family in the Modern World*), Pope John Paul II states: "Today's family in the Western world is in crisis. The widespread practice of unnatural contraception, a decreasing birth rate, a rising divorce rate, a greater tolerance of pre-marital sex and adultery, sterilization and abortion, a confusion of sex roles in combination with a decline in parental authority comprise a list of contributing factors resulting in a deterioration of family life."[2] More recently he has provided us with a beautiful meditation on the dignity of woman's vocation.[3] At the present time, in Western society, most religious communities are endeavoring to increase their numbers, while many, if not most Christian families are limiting the size of their families to only a few children who are not spaced at the natural rate of about two years between births. Such a situation is bound to have an adverse effect on the total number of young people entering the religious life.

In his recent book *The Incarnation in a Divided World*, Donald DeMarco presents the basic doctrine of the incarnation as it relates to the serious problems faced by the world today: nature, love, education, the media, contraception, pornography, parenthood, vocations and Mary's motherhood.[4] The author, like an experienced thinking (not pill-prescribing) physician, has made an accurate diagnosis of the disorder and prescribes sound therapeutic programs for the ultimate recovery of his patient. I quote here a few statements from his work that directly relate to the purpose of publishing this book.

The Incarnation—God descending into the life of man—is so startling a doctrine that the modern world, given its pride and commitment to success, finds it impossible to understand, let alone believe.

Christianity demands humility and an affection for littleness. "The mark of the Christian," wrote Bishop Sheen, "is the willingness to look for the Divine in the flesh of a babe in a crib, the continuing Christ under the appearance of bread on an altar, and a meditation and a prayer on a string of beads."

Christianity entered the world because a woman was willing to make a child the center of her life. Religion must have a descending arc before it can have an upward swing. It is like an inverted rainbow in which the fall precedes the rise. It is not difficult to understand why the ambitious and self-centered are often irreligious. Christianity invites us to lower ourselves so that we can uplift people. This is exactly what God does through the Incarnation.

In eighteenth-century France, aristocratic and socially ambitious mothers sent their children off to country wet-nurses, thereby liberating themselves so that they might establish salons and invent epigrams. Today's liberated mother fancies she has much more important things to do than to stay home and involve herself in a round of changing diapers, picking up toys, and making meals. 'Make policy, not coffee,' reads the feminist's liberation button. Inevitably, however, the coffee makers must labor outside the penumbra of respectability.

In order to use nature, man must first understand and obey her. The sixteenth-century philosopher Francis Bacon, at the very dawn of the scientific revolution, knew with superlative insight that 'nature to be commanded must be obeyed.'

Medical technology, which formerly restricted itself to co-operating with nature, is now involved in modifying man's body. But the more we are isolated from our own bodies, the more we lose touch with the world of nature and grace with which we are united through our bodies.

Our deeper need is not for our bodies to be altered by technology, but for our selves to be healed by grace. And the first thing we must do in order to prepare ourselves to receive the grace which is made available to us through the intermediary of nature is to be whole, that is, to be an integrated unity of body and soul, nature and spirit.

The fullness of both mother-and fatherhood demands the unification of procreation and bodified, conjugal love. As this unity is compromised or violated, the moral and spiritual meaning of mother-and fatherhood are proportionally jeopardized.[5]

I would like to draw attention to another book, one which demonstrates in couples' own words how they joyfully live the truths of *Humanae Vitae: Challenge of Love* by Mary Shivanandan. One couple who switched from using the "Pill" to natural conception regulation comments: "It was the first time we really heard the Church's position. The Roman Catholic Church is not against birth control, but for a natural relationship for the couple. I call it taking control out of the laboratory and giving it to our relationship. That's when we both began to get excited about natural methods."[6]

As an older father and grandfather, I would like to end this discussion of the Roman Catholic position on birth control by quoting from Malcolm Muggeridge, whose experience confirms my own:

> One thing that I know will appear in social histories in the future is that the dissolution in our way of life relates directly to the matter that is raised in *Humanae Vitae*. The journalists, the media write and hold forth about the various elements in the crisis of the Western world today; about inflation, about overpopulation, about pending energy shortages, about detente, about hundreds of things. But they

overlook the distortion and abuse of what should be the essential creativity of men and women, enriching their lives, as it has and does enrich people's lives, and when they are as old as I am, enriches them particularly beautifully—when they see as they depart from this world their grandchildren beginning the process of living which they are ending. There is no beauty, there is no joy, there is no compensation that anything could offer in the way of leisure, of so-called freedom from domestic duties, which could possibly compensate for a thousandth part of the joy that an old man feels when he sees this beautiful thing: life beginning again as his ends, in those children that have come into the world through his love and through a marriage which has lasted through fifty and more years. I assure you that what I say to you is true, and that when you are that age there is nothing in the way of honors, in the way of variety, in the way of so-called freedom, which could come within a thousandth part of measuring up to that wonderful sense of having been used as an instrument, not in the achievement of some stupid kind of personal erotic excitement, but in the realization of this wonderful thing—human procreation.

Now of course, when *Humanae Vitae* was published to the world and was set upon by all the pundits of the media, it was attacked as being a failure to sympathize with the difficulties of young people getting married. That was the basis on which the attack was mounted. But it was perfectly obvious that contraception was something that would just not stop with limiting families; that, in fact, it would lead inevitably, as night follows day, to abortion and then euthanasia. But it was quite obvious that this would be so. If you once accepted the idea that the erotic satisfaction was itself a justification, then you had to accept also the idea that if erotic satisfaction led to pregnancy, then the person concerned was entitled to have the pregnancy stopped. And, of course, we had abortion bills that swept through the whole Western world where there now virtually exists abortion on demand. The result has been an enormous increase in the misery and unhappiness of individual human beings and, most tragically, the enormous weakening of the family.[6]

Notes

1. John Paul II, *Reflections on Humanae Vitae*. Boston: St. Paul Editions, 1984.

2. John Paul II, *Familiaris Consortio: The Role of the Christian Family in the Modern World*. Boston: St. Paul Editions, 1981.

3. John Paul II, *Dignitate Mulieris*. Boston: St. Paul Editions, 1988.

4. Donald DeMarco, *The Incarnation in a Divided World*. Front Royal: Christian College Press, 1988.

5. Mary Shivanandan, *Challenge to Love*. Bethesda: KM Associates, 1988.

6. Malcolm Muggeridge, Personal communication, 1988.

Chapter 9

A Pediatrician's Advice
for Family Life

It has been the author's observation, after over fifty years of clinical pediatric experience and fifty years of marriage, that to establish enduring families in our increasingly complex society, it is equally important for both boys and girls to complete their formal basic education and to become self-sufficient before marriage. True marriage is much more than a simple love affair; it is a firm commitment involving the sacrifice of one's ego in a relationship in which a man and woman choose to become and remain one forever. After marriage, both will have grave family responsibilities requiring sacrifices for each other. The boy should be a man in a position to support a family and with a basic knowledge of reproductive physiology. The girl should be a mature woman with knowledge of her fertility and with sufficient education to support herself and her children should the need arise.

Soon after marriage, it is desirable for most couples to *prove* their fertility and establish a family. Children normally bind and bring couples closer together and help them to mature faster. My extensive clinical experience with families leads me to conclude that sex without children does not get marriages off to a good start, and is more likely to lead to self-indulgence. *Spacing of children at about two-year intervals is desirable. This can be achieved by ecological breast-feeding and knowledge of fertility awareness.* After a couple has the number of children they can support and educate, a natural method of conception regulation can and should be used effectively to control conceptions. These natural, safe, free and reliable methods require education, experience, and above all, the motivation of both husband and wife. *Natural family planning can be as effective as any unnatural method.*

As a pediatrician, my concern has been to help parents accept, love and enjoy their children by learning and understanding good health practices. It is my conviction that more than anything else, children need unselfish parents. A *full-time* mother and a responsible and loving father are essential for children, especially in infancy and the critical preschool years when physical, emotional and intellectual growth and development are proceeding so rapidly.

The stages of child development are the same today as they have always been, although the rate of development varies depending on various environmental factors. Physical growth and development are commonly measured by observing the increase in height and weight and the improvement of muscular coordination. For example, a child may be observed to be growing larger and going through the stages of creeping, toddling, walking and running. As infants grow, they gradually become aware that they are independent human beings with minds and wills of their own. In order to be happy, they must learn how to use help from others in order to gain self-control without losing self-esteem. A child's emotional pattern becomes fairly well established during infancy and the early years of life. Thereafter, it becomes progressively more difficult to alter the pattern as the child grows older. The emotional health of the child invariably reflects the emotional health of the parents.

Every child has a great need for security, happiness, affection and applause, as well as for *discipline*. Gradually, a child needs to learn to assume responsibilities in keeping with her or his age. On occasion, all children will intentionally do something which they know is wrong or neglect to do something which they know they should do. At these times, punishment should be carried out immediately. It is of equal importance that the parent forgive and forget after the punishment has been given. Children are reared in a world of discipline and obedience, as they are necessarily dependent on others, but gradually, especially during adolescence, this state of dependence has to be transcended so that ultimately they can become self-disciplined, autonomous and mature adults. They need to learn to live not in dependency but with self-responsibiilty. Children who never cross this threshold remain adolescents even during their adulthood.

During adolescence there is a great need for self-expression and independence, and a strong desire to be like other members of one's peer group. Any limitation is "troublesome" for adolescents, and their desire to follow the crowd is often in conflict with what they have been taught at home, school and church. However, the problems of adolescents can be prevented or mitigated to a great extent if ample opportunities are given for self-direction as the child matures and demonstrates the capacity for autonomy. As indicated in the following statements, many authorities agree that for optimal development, a child needs one person as a full-time caretaker for the early years of life.

According to Maria Montessori:

> It is not paradoxical to say that, while adults suffer among the poor, children suffer among the rich. Apart from the complications of clothing, of social custom, of the crowds of friends and relatives that visit the baby, it happens that in the moneyed class the mother often entrusts her child to a wet-nurse, or seeks other means of release, while the mother in poor circumstances follows the path of nature and keeps the child at her side. In a number of small ways we are led to see that things the adult world values can have reversed effects in the world of children. But let us think, for a moment, of the many peoples of the world who live at different cultural levels from our own. In the matter of child rearing, almost all of these seem to become more enlightened than ourselves—with all our Western ultra-modern ideals. Nowhere else, in fact, do we find children treated in a fashion so opposed to their natural needs.
>
> In almost all countries, the baby accompanies his mother wherever she goes. Mother and child are inseparable . . . mother and child are one. Except where civilization has broken down this custom, no mother ever entrusts her child to someone else.[1]

According to Horst Schetelig, M.D.:

> Children always need time. If the mother and the parents are not prepared to put themselves at the disposal of the child and his needs in the first years of life, much more time will be mercilessly demanded subsequently. . . . If in the first years of life there is enough time to devote oneself to the baby, to be there for him, to later build, read, and romp with him, these children are not only content, but by means of the love enriched through the play and through the joy and the task itself, they learn to occupy themselves intensively and to stick to tasks—factors which are urgently required at school. All those things which do not have to be laboriously repeated. During the first three years the child should stay with his mother. The younger the child, the more he needs his mother. Working parents often give only one, two, or three hours a day when the young child needs eight to nine hours.[2]

According to Harold M. Voth, M.D. (senior psychiatrist at the Menninger Foundation):

> A baby must have a mother who is mature enough to attend to its needs and provide so-called object constancy for a minimum of three years. The very foundation of personality is created during this period. The mothering function during these critical years is one of the most important of all human events but, unfortunately, one of the least appreciated or regarded by society.[3]

According to the Bureau of Labor Statistics, in 1984, 49.5% of all mothers with children under one year of age were working outside the home. That was an increase of 24% since 1970, before which time the Bureau kept no similar figures. Shortly thereafter, an advisory panel at Yale University concluded after a year-long study that babies and families were being adversely affected as a result of the pressure on mothers to return too early to jobs their families depended upon. "The child really needs a base, the two important parents. If they have to spread the base too thin, we worry about whether the children will ever be able to nurture their own children, whether they will be able to think of other people first, rather than themselves, whether there's a sort of chaos later on for kids who haven't developed a basic sense of trust."[4]

In modern societies, couples from more educated and affluent families have tended to marry later, to use unnatural methods of birth control in order to avoid conceptions and to have only one or two children. In recent years, increasing numbers of mothers have become aware of the desirability of breast-feeding and nurse their infants, although only for a few months. However, many if not most couples in more affluent families have generally lacked the determination to make the financial and social sacrifices required to have the mother available full-time to nurse each baby for the space of about a year and to provide the daily care and education of their rapidly developing preschool-age children. It is often diffi-cult for many fathers to provide full financial support of the family unless both parents are capable of and willing to distinguish be-tween necessities and luxuries and to live on a more limited in-come by making major modifications of their lifestyles. In addition to a full-time mother, infants and preschool children also need a loving father, not only to support and help the mother but also to demonstrate by his actions that he loves their mother.

The first child in any family has inexperienced parents, but if the child is wanted and accepted, the parents learn a great deal in a very short period of time. A second child, arriving in about two years, will not only extend the education of the parents but will automatically provide the discipline especially needed by a first child. Three or more children, spaced at approximate two-year in-tervals, are desirable for most healthy couples living in a stable environment. Ultimately, each couple needs to make the grave de-cision as to how many children they can care for and raise, but with full knowledge of the value of children to each other and in later life. Many mothers have told me they do not understand why their third child is so "good" and such a joy. The simple answer is that the third child and future children have experienced parents as well as older sisters and/or brothers. Parents with larger families do not divide their love, they multiply it. The distinctive but coop-erative help of mothers and fathers in families provides their chil-dren with ideal role models for normal gender identification during infancy and the critical preschool years.

As reviewed in Chapter 6, increased medical knowledge of reproductive physiology has recently made possible a more complete understanding of natural family planning. These new, more precise natural methods of controlling births are reliable, safe, and inexpensive, and they also help protect the health of mothers- and grandmothers-to-be. Natural family planning involves the couple in a whole new approach to conception regulation in which the normal and natural processes of fertility are understood, accepted and lived with, rather than being disrupted by expensive chemicals, pills, intrauterine devices or surgery, all of which have real potential for causing very serious health problems for women. Because of the shared commitment of the couple "to be responsible together" for their shared fertility, greater mutual respect and trust develops. Parents who learn and practice natural conception regulation are preparing themselves to become the most effective teachers of human sexuality for their own children and thereby for all succeeding generations.

As an experienced family doctor, I urge a return to the trustworthy traditional values and teachings that held families together, that is, a sense of personal responsibility and dignity, including chastity before and fidelity after marriage. But concurrently we need to accept that unless religious leaders begin to reaffirm in a meaningful way the traditional Christian condemnation of unnatural methods of birth control, young and middle-aged adults will not alter established patterns, overcome social pressures and accept the self-discipline required for natural methods of fertility regulation. We also need to appreciate fully that *reliable* natural methods of conception regulation only began to emerge in the late 1960s and into societies which for a generation or two had accepted and practiced unnatural but legally approved methods of birth control, usually on the encouragement and advice of doctors. These unnatural methods were either sanctioned or left up to the individual conscience by many (if not most) religious teachers, notwithstanding the consistent official teaching of marital chastity by the Catholic church.

In spite of the confusion that has resulted from this unfortunate state of affairs, I wish to emphasize that there is great potential for educating future generations. Our children are our reservoir of hope. Concurrent with their sexual maturation, adolescents deserve to be taught the importance and values of family life, of the full range of natural conception regulation, including the priceless value of chastity before marriage and the practice of periodic abstinence from sexual intercourse within marriage. Consequently the most urgent need is to develop programs to help parents meet their grave responsibilities in this regard. Family life education is the process by which the family transmits values from one generation to succeeding generations.

We live in a dynamic world, and each generation faces new and different problems. In the more developed world, as the general health and nutritional status of children has improved, the age of maturation has decreased. Over the past few generations, the age for girls to begin menstruating has gradually decreased from over 16 to under 13 years of age. Boys are also developing sexually at earlier ages (13–16 years). We need to make a clear distinction between so-called sex education and sexuality education. Human sexuality includes emotional and spiritual maturation in addition to an understanding of the facts of reproductive physiology. It is not surprising that merely teaching reproductive physiology and the use of contraceptives to adolescents has not been effective in controlling teen-age pregnancies and even repeated pregnancies among our youth.

Our children are growing up in a secularized society which accepts and even condones sexual activity as an end in itself, and outside the context of marriage. A carefree emphasis on the pleasures of sexual activity ignores moral constructs and reduces consciousness that the misuse of sex invariably leads to very serious and lasting problems. Many studies reveal why simply giving contraceptives to teenagers is ineffectual. Such an approach only exacerbates the classical characteristics of adolescents: immaturity; high-impulse gratification drives; poor communication abilities; and the lack of long-term committed relationships. Knowing all about reproduction in no way prepares the teenager to deal effectively with passion, arousal and self-discipline. During the period of sexual maturation (which primarily occurs when children are in secondary schools), the greatest need is for them to learn how to cope with their normal sexual drives. Although it is primarily the parents' responsibility to teach their children human sexuality, at present, most parents are not prepared to do this, and do not have adequate church and community resources to help them. Parents who use unnatural methods of birth control themselves are in a "compromised position" to instruct and guide their children to accept chastity. Most parents and grandparents of former generations taught and firmly believed in chastity before marriage and fidelity after marriage. Only two or three generations ago, chastity before marriage and fidelity after marriage were the accepted norms of most societies. However, within the past few generations many national cultures have undergone rapid profound changes, so that now unnatural methods of contraception and abortion are not only legal, but are advocated as the new societal norms for responsible sex and responsible parenthood.

Providing contraceptives for teenagers is tantamount to encouraging them to indulge in premarital sex. Instead of this ineffectual non-approach, sexuality education at home, school and church should be premised on self-control and chastity. All adolescents find the struggle for self-mastery difficult. Giving contraceptives to adolescents is equivalent to telling them that they cannot and need not control their sexual desires. As might be expected, the increased exposure of teenagers to contraceptives and education in their use has also led to more promiscuity (now euphemistically called more "sexual activity"), and to more pregnancies and abortions. Greater promiscuity has also resulted in an increase in venereal diseases, including the fatal disease AIDS, and to involuntary sterility which robs many young women of their greatest creative power, the gift of motherhood. Parents urgently need high-quality family life educational resources to teach their children human sexuality.

To explain my own views on family life education, I quote from Ingrid Trobisch's 1984 address to the International Federation for Family Promotion:

A. What is family life education?

Helping men and women understand each other, giving help to parents in raising their children wisely, and making changes in our society through healthily contagious living.

B. When does family life education begin?

Long before the birth of the child . . . especially influenced by the way the parents themselves were raised. Is the child viewed as a nuisance, or only as an heir, or as a real, healthy individual to be loved and guided?

C. Pregnancy, childbirth, and breast-feeding:

The child in the womb is dependent on the health of the mother. The moment of birth should be the time of a woman's greatest dignity, when she is a co-worker with God in bringing this new life into the visible world . . . . Newborn babies need food, warmth, and security, and all three are received best at the mother's breast, where the foundation for mutual confidence and companionship is begun.

D. The place of the father in family life education:

The father is the first man that a daughter knows, and he to a great extent determines her attitude toward men later in life . . . . The father is the role model for the son; the daughter needs a mother with whom she can identify.

E. The role of parents in preschool education:

The foundations for self-esteem and self-acceptance, essential for any love relationship, are laid by parents. Children need to know that they are unique, created in the image of God . . . . Answer all questions simply and naturally, but do not tell more than the child asks . . . .

F. The role of parents in the school years of their children:

Example speaks louder than words . . . . The school child needs kindness ("I'm on your side"), encouragement ("You can do it"), and challenge ("Now, do it") . . . . The family table conversation can be the greatest single influence in the life of the child.

G. The role of parents during the adolescent years:

This is the time for teaching the child that it is possible to live a fulfilled life in spite of many unfulfilled desires . . . . Adolescents need help to understand their own physical and emotional development and to apprehend the values of sexual activity within the context of a mature, committed love relationship.

H. Mature unselfish parents are needed to accomplish

family life education goals. A child is not a toy, but a very real person to be respected, loved, and educated. Our goal is reached when we see our children establishing stable families and doing a good job of parenting.[5]

As a finale, I will synthesize the prescriptions which I see as essential for teaching our youth the values of living in harmony with nature. From infancy, children (especially adolescents) need role models and factual information to help them understand why and how to cope with their normal sexual desires, and how the abuse of sex can lead to very serious problems. After marriage, couples should prove their fertility, and then space their children about two years apart by ecological breast-feeding and fertility awareness. Both parents need to understand that during pregnancy and for about a year when the baby is truly breast-fed, the wife does not ovulate, so conceptions are controlled naturally. Consequently, during the early years of married life, sexual abstinence is limited primarily to times of illness or separation and to a short period between births. The period of involutionary changes after birth in a healthy woman is shortened considerably by natural birth and by ecological breast-feeding. When the couple decides to widen the spacing or to stop having more children, conception regulation by natural family planning will still permit them to have new honeymoons every month. After only a few years they will begin to recognize the symptoms and signs of approaching menopause, and before long the wife will become naturally sterile, with a great likelihood of having intact female organs. Sexual abstinence is much less difficult for a mature unselfish couple with a secure family life.

Notes

1. Maria Montessori, *The Child in the Family*. Chicago: Henry Regnery Company, Chicago, 1970.

2. Schetelig, H. Personal communication, 1980.

3. Voth, H. M. and M. H. *Psychotherapy and the Role of the Environment*. New York: Behavioral Publishing, 1973.

4. Zigler, E. F. and Frank, M. *The Parental Leave Crisis: Toward a National Policy*. New Haven: Yale University Press, 1988.

5. Ingrid Trobish, *Family Life Education: Selected Papers*. (International Federation for Family Life Promotion). Hong Kong: Caxton Graphic Press, 1984.

Chapter 10

A Physician's "Word" to the Health Professions

The scientific data presented in the previous chapters confirms the importance of good nutrition and physical fitness for women before and during pregnancy; the desirability of natural labor and delivery for healthy women; the immediate needs of the mother and her newborn baby for tactile contact immediately after birth; the emotional, nutritive, immunological and fertility regulation advantages of ecological breast-feeding for a year or more after birth, and the availability of reliable, cost-free, safe natural methods of conception regulation when needed to control the size of families.

When properly interpreted, understood and applied, advances in knowledge extend human freedom, but improperly understood and used, they restrict personal freedom and tend to enslave. The objective of this book on human ecology is to envision what is attainable if the recent advances in scientific knowledge are better understood and applied for the welfare of the family. The vision also must include an awareness of the inequality in the distribution of the benefits of science and technology. In the more developed areas of the world, the family, the most vital and basic human institution, is being adversely affected by profound and rapid changes resulting from the adoption of artificial ways of life. In turn, the more developed world is introducing and financing these detrimental changes in the developing areas of the world.

We are now faced with the difficult task of re-educating the health professionals who have been taught and are now accustomed to and experienced in the use of unnatural practices. Unfortunately, in the past, most physicians' education and clinical training were directed primarily toward understanding, detecting, and treating pathological conditions (disease states) rather than toward a better understanding of physiological (natural) processes and the use of preventive health practices to appreciate and support more fully the wisdom of nature.[1] Therefore, physicians have been conditioned by training, example, and experience to intervene and disrupt natural processes. Such interventions are more common in obstetrics and pediatrics because to a great extent these specialities are concerned with the preventive care of healthy women and children. For example, episiotomies are easily done when doctors are delivering shaved, anesthetized, positioned and surgically draped women in hospital delivery rooms. Episiotomies have become a nearly routine hospital obstetrical procedure, although they cause the mother considerable discomfort after parturition. In pediatrics, supplemental formula feedings, pacifiers, and the too-early introduction of other foods are recommended, which rapidly disrupt ecological breast-feeding. These evolutions have occurred because such interventions provide quick and easy "solutions" rather than the somewhat more time-consuming but preferable natural ways to resolve problems.

Originally, the ethical basis for the practice of therapeutic medicine was to identify pathological states and insofar as possible to restore them to normal. Preventive medicine seeks to discover the causes of different disorders in order to prevent them from occurring. By disrupting natural processes in healthy persons, the medical profession has relinquished the traditional basic principle of medical practice which was, "First, to do no harm."[2]

By the middle of the twentieth century, an ever-increasing number of the health professions began to accept barrier forms of unnatural conception control for limited reasons. At present, many if not most physicians and other health providers endorse numerous convenient but more hazardous methods to prevent ovulation or implantation, or to cause abortion or sterilization. That is, birth control pills and IUDs are advocated for healthy women in order to induce an abnormal (pathological) state; this is done even in young girls without their parents' consent. New birth control pills are currently being developed and used experimentally either to prevent implantation of the embryo or to cause a medical abortion directly. The repeated use of such potent medications will most assuredly cause serious short-and long-term physical complications as well as very serious psychological and social problems. The current erroneous concept is that more effective contraceptive measures are preferable to more abortions.

Because of the perceived need to modify population growth rates, many well-intentioned people are degrading the value of human procreation. There is great truth in Solzenitsyn's pronouncement that "the West has lost its will to live." This is a grave problem. An ever-increasing number of educated, dedicated families are needed to raise and educate their own children, as well as to teach the deprived segments of the population how to live with dignity and adjust the size of their families according to their ability to care for them and to provide an improved family life.

A major factor impeding progress toward the long-term goals of meeting children's needs is that far too many couples who could best afford to have and care for more children are having very few children or none at all, and they sincerely believe that it is desirable to persuade or even coerce the deprived segments of society to do the same. Children are also needed and wanted by economically and socially disadvantaged couples, as children provide their greatest joy and hopes for the future.

To be effective teachers of natural methods, it is highly desirable for health workers not only to understand but also to practice what they are teaching. Ironically, evidence is accumulating that the underprivileged segments of society who have less formal education are more receptive to natural childbirth and to learning and practicing natural child-spacing (requiring ecological breast-feeding and periodic abstinence) than are the more affluent segments of society who have more formal education. Observation of human ecology in the international setting discloses similar patterns. Since economic survival in underdeveloped agricultural communities has depended upon the contribution of children both during childhood and as adults, large families have traditionally been considered a necessity in areas of the world with a high infant mortality rate and more primitive agricultural methods. Motivation for "population control" depends upon demonstrating that infant mortality can be reduced by improved public health programs and that food production can be increased by more effective agricultural methods. Couples with limited economic resources are easily motivated to limit the size of their families as soon as they realize that most of their children will survive and that their social security will be more dependent on how well they provide for and educate fewer children, rather than on how many children they have.

Pregnancy outcome as well as marital and child-rearing patterns are associated closely with socioeconomic and cultural factors. Adolescent girls from insecure homes are likely to conceive premaritally or marry adolescent boys at a very early age, be poorly educated and become fatigued from poor eating and sleeping habits. They have "poorly born" infants with short birth intervals, give too little attention to preventive health practices, and, together with their children, they become a costly ongoing burden to the community's therapeutic health services. Infants and young children from these families have more frequent and severe infections, often requiring hospital care. Since a high percentage of their infants have been deprived of colostrum and human milk, they are less resistant to infections. Most of these insecure and often single mothers have never been taught the advantages of breast-feeding. In the United States, many of these mothers also find it imperative for economic reasons to resume work outside their homes within a few weeks after delivery. Consequently, many of their young infants are placed under the care of others, frequently in substandard facilities and with increased exposure to infections.

In contrast to the younger girls from more deprived segments of society, women from more affluent families are more likely to marry later, use unnatural methods of birth control to avoid all conception, or to have only one or two children "unnaturally" spaced. Many of these women who use contraceptives, especially

IUDs and birth control pills, become infertile and will find it very difficult to adopt an infant. The infants from more affluent families are often delivered by technologically-directed methods, including a high percentage of caesarean sections. In recent years, increasing numbers of these mothers are informed and aware of the desirability of breast-feeding and are nursing their infants, but only for a few months—which, as we noted earlier, is not an effective means of natural conception regulation.

Artificial birth control is now being subsidized by many private and governmental agencies and has rapidly become very big business. Many thousands of people are now funded by these agencies. In 1977, it was estimated that worldwide, about 55 million women were taking birth control pills, about 15 million had IUDs, and 65 million were using other forms of artificial birth control. If 55 million women are taking birth control pills, a conservative estimated annual return to pharmaceutical firms alone would no doubt exceed $1.5 billion. To the costs of these drugs must be added additional billions of dollars paid to doctors and other health professionals for prescribing and distributing birth control pills, inserting and extracting IUDs and doing sterilizations and surgical abortions.

In 1985, Slacks and Hilgers estimated the cost of advertising to promote artificial methods of birth control versus advertising to promote fertility enhancement in the five leading academic journals of obstetrics and gynecology. The total cost of advertisements in 1983 for ablating or destroying fertility was estimated to be $1,751,097—or 26% of the total advertising revenues. In contrast, the cost of advertisements aimed at enhancing fertility was only $281,870. The ratio of space allotted was 5 to 1. They also estimated that the cost of prescriptions for oral contraceptives, written in 1983 by obstetricians only, was $272 million.[3]

The total cost of supporting these artificial methods to control population is staggering, and it does not take into account the costs of the adverse effects of these methods on the health of millions of women. Consider what might be accomplished if only a part of these funds were diverted to support maternal and child health clinics to improve the nutritional state of mothers and to teach safe methods of natural family planning, including ecological breast-feeding. Natural conception regulation is inexpensive, and it avoids undermining the health of the women who comprise the most vital members (the heart) of all families.

More private and governmental resources are needed to educate families regarding the importance of good nutritional practices, especially of women before and during the childbearing years; and the education of youth before and after marriage regarding the advantages of ecological breast-feeding and natural conception and fertility regulation. These preventive health services are needed especially in the depressed areas of the more developed world and throughout the developing world.

United Nations reports indicate that in over 100 developing countries, poverty, illiteracy and hunger disrupt the daily lives of millions of children. Many of these families live in absolute poverty, without health care and with no access to clean water or proper sanitation. Infants in these families who are breast-fed during infancy are five to ten times less likely to die early in life. Heat-stable vaccines are now available which do not require refrigeration and are relatively inexpensive. Accurate growth monitoring is also inexpensive, and if properly done and interpreted will detect early signs of malnutrition or ill health. Oral rehydration using salt and sugar solutions can be effectively taught and used for diarrhea, the great killer of infants in the developing world.

In 1925, Mahatma Gandhi made the following prophetic statement: "I urge the advocates of artificial methods of birth control to consider the consequences. Any large use of the methods is likely to result in the dissolution of the marriage bond and in free love."

Marriages in the United States are characterized by their dissolubility—for every marriage that lasts, another fails. Nearly two out of every three remarriages ends in failure. Couples are no longer taught to understand the sacrificial nature of real love: that it requires "giving up" things. Too often so-called self-actualization movements lead to ego satisfaction and selfishness. Consequently, incompatibility abounds. Since about 1960 there has been considerable evidence that our national culture has been influenced more by national television (usually devoid of moral content) than by families, churches, and educational institutions. Consequently, we are faced with serious moral and ethical problems.

Demographic trends are rapidly upsetting the underpinnings of the traditional family. This is evident in data recently published by the United States National Center for Health Statistics, as reviewed and reported by the American Academy of Pediatrics.[4]

On each day, on the average, in 1984, 10,052 babies were born in the United States. Of these 10,052 babies born each day:

—2,111 were born to unmarried women;
—121 were born to women under the age of 15;
—3,126 were born to women under the age of 19;
—686 were born with low birthweights;
—503 were born to women who did not receive prenatal care at all or until after their third trimester of pregnancy;
—19 were born suffering from fetal alcohol syndrom;
—108 died, 70 of which were neo-natal deaths; 38 were postnatal deaths.

Each day, on the average, in the United States in 1986:

—there were 3,477 legal abortions;
—5,715 cases of child abuse were reported, of which 2,019 were substantiated;
—7 children or adolescents were homicide victims;
—3 children died from non-intentional gunshot wounds;
—5 teenagers commited suicide.

However, in spite of these sobering statistics, there is hope, as we are beginning to hear pleas for a return to the values and practices that traditionally held families together and contributed to a more stable society; that is, a sense of personal responsibility and dignity, including chastity before and fidelity after marriage. Our best hope for the future is to help parents educate their children who are on their way toward marriage and family life and thereby to help each new generation to better appreciate the many advantages of living a more natural way of life. We need to resign ourselves to the fact that it will be very difficult for young and middle-aged adults to alter established patterns and to overcome social pressures that seek easy technological "solutions," and to learn biological methods, including natural childbirth, ecological breast-feeding, and other natural methods of fertility regulation. However, there is great hope for teaching future generations. Therefore, educators should direct their attention primarily to helping the health professions and parents meet this grave responsibility.

A return to natural family planning in all of its aspects offers the best hope of overcoming the sense of foreboding for the future resulting from the moral vacuum that is enveloping our civilization. A new, more peaceful era could be attained if the scientific discoveries and technological advances now available were applied to constructive rather than destructive purposes, and if world resources were distributed on the basis of social justice in order to permit the emergence of a truly ecological society. In recent years, there has been an increasing realization that the delivery of health services to families has developed with far too little understanding of biological and emotional needs. Observation and experience should teach physicians and other health workers that interfering with natural processes in healthy persons invariably results, sooner or later, in varying degrees of detectable pathological changes. Human ecology concerns not only communities and nations, but also the basic primary unit of society, that is, the family. Our long-term objective should be to have stable families with healthy children. There will never be too many well-cared-for children in the world, for in them resides the real hope for a more peaceful future.

Notes

1. J. N. Santa Marie, "The Social Effects of Contraception," *Linacre Quarterly* 5: 2, 114–127, May, 1984.

2. In 1976, a book entitled *First Do No Harm* related the experience of a young woman who died of cancer induced by birth control pills. Posthumously, she won a court settlement against the manufacturers of the pills. Her story was told by her mother. *First Do No Harm*. New York: Sun River Press, 1976.

3. R. M. Slacks and T. W. Hilgers, "Advertising Trends in Major Journals of Obstetrics and Gynecology," *Natural Family Planning* 9: 4, pp. 292–305, 1985.

4. National Center for Health Statistics, Washington, D.C., 1988.

Epilogue

by Herbert Ratner, M. D.

I know of no academician who has utilized his emeritus years more meritoriously and worthily than Dr. Robert Jackson. Not only was he a proponent of breast-feeding from his early days as a pediatric resident at the University of Iowa, he has also been alert to the excessive increase of caesarian operations *in primipara*. He has also been aware of the victimization of women by the modern contraceptives which unreflective gynecologists have doled out to them as safe. While planned parenthooders, social engineers, and profit-hungry drug companies and device manufacturers were also pushing contraceptives, Dr. Jackson seized upon the "ecological" concept as an intergrating principle for a sane and salutary guide to wholesome family life.

He opted for an approach to reproduction based on the design and norms of nature to which mammalian inclinations implanted by nature lead us, and which are confirmed by reason. Reason makes it possible for man to read the book of nature and abstract its wisdom. Accordingly he espouses a natural reproductive trinity: natural childbirth, natural infant nurturing, and the use of natural conception regulation. In so doing he gives shape to the uprising of the female consumer against male-dominated technology.

Not unrelated to the genesis of Jackson's *magnum opus* is the fact that the author was a 1934 medical school graduate of the University of Michigan, which at the time was noted for its great European-educated teachers, bearers of the Hippocratic tradition.

Nor is it unrelated that a small group of his classmates became part
of Jackson's subsequent personal and professional life. One classmate, now a well-known Trappist psychiatrist and spiritual director, Fr. Raphael Simon, wrote the introduction to this book and
another classmate, myself, has written this epilogue. Jackson's
roommate at medical school, John Hillabrand of Toledo, became a
brilliant practicing obstetrician, a leading authority and teacher of
the sympto-thermal method and eventually an expert witness on
oral contraceptive court cases. Dr. Jackson also founded, along
with this writer and several other physicians, the National Commission on Human Life, Reproduction and Rhythm, an organization which pioneered national and international conferences on
sympto-thermic rhythm from 1967 through 1971. Finally, there was
classmate Dorothy Smith (Ratner), who taught us physiology and
who later devoted most of her life to teaching her husband (this
writer) and others what family life was all about. In later years all
of the foregoing members of the Class of 1934 were closely associated with the work of *Child and Family Quarterly* in its exposition of
the teachings of nature concerning family life. Drs. Jackson, Hillabrand and Ratner served as editors, while the other two medical
classmates were editorial advisors.

We, his long-time friends and colleagues, are particularly in-
debted to Dr. Jackson for undertaking and completing this much-
needed book. He brought to the laborious task of writing the
dedication and perseverance of a crusader convinced of the need
of our sick society to recover nature's wisdom in the crucial area of
family life. He not only researched the literature but also persever-
ingly sought the advice and consensus of experts working in the
field of fertility awareness and in the role of periodic abstinence in
marriage.

But more than this, he brought to the book the knowledge and
experience of a personal and professional life well spent. Prefes-
sionally he has been an international and honored authority on
child growth and juvenile diabetes. As the long-time chairman of
pediatrics at the University of Missouri, his greatest contribution,
perhaps, was to send forth to all corners of the earth thirty-six
trained pediatricians with a special commitment to community

services. Through his guidance, a dozen went to the Middle East, and others to Chile, Brazil, Mexico, Indochina and Africa, as well as a sprinkling to European countries. He was a visiting professor at the American University in Beirut during the academic year 1962–1963.

His residents and other students gained more than a specialty education. They benefited by working under a committed son of God. Although he taught at secular universities for over fifty years, Dr. Jackson never compromised his Catholic faith. When an occasion for teaching arose, he never hesitated to communicate the fact that God was a friend of both physician and patient. When I flew to Columbia to attend his retirement banquet as Chairman of the Pediatrics Department, I was greatly impressed by the anecdotes of former residents who invariably made reference to his religious commitment.

At the personal level he has had an exemplary family life. The best measure of his worth was the self-effacing woman whom he chose as his partner in life and who nurtured their seven children. Since his first six children were girls (the seventh was a boy), Dr. Jackson benefited (as all males do) from the special insights in life which a man gets from mother, wife and daughters. Perhaps God graced Bob Jackson's marriage with an abundance of daughters to help his book be as good as it is.

Some closing thoughts are in order to round out this epilogue. There are pitfalls on the road of life. Kierkegaard observed one major one: "the trouble with life is that we understand it backwards, but have to live it forwards." Thus the last half of life, yet to be lived, tells us more about what is important in life than does the first half. Here, we must look to the accumulated wisdom of mankind. From the vantage point of one who has traversed the second half of life, I offer a few thoughts which came to mind after reading Dr. Jackson's superb book.

The child is a gift both biologically and theologically. One must be cautious about rejecting gifts, since one can't always have them on demand. The greatest gift one can give a present child or children is another brother or sister. In the Judeo-Christian tradition, the virtue of prudence includes in its judgment hope and confidence in the providential order. One must be careful not to outsmart oneself by attempting to substitute man's plan for God's plan. Lastly, one should remember when things do not turn out as planned, that sometimes the best things in life are unplanned. That is what an advent is all about.

—